# THE BARBANELL REPORT

*Books by Paul Beard*

SURVIVAL OF DEATH
LIVING ON
HIDDEN MAN

# THE
# BARBANELL REPORT

*transmitted to*
MARIE CHERRIE

*edited and with an Introduction by*
PAUL BEARD

PILGRIM  BOOKS
TASBURGH NORWICH ENGLAND

Copyright © Paul Beard 1987

British Library Cataloguing in Publication Data
Barbanell, Maurice *(Spirit)*
   The Barbanell report.
   1. Spirit writings
   I. Title    II. Cherrie, Marie
   133.9'3         BF1301

   ISBN 0–946259–23–2

Photoset by Waveney Typesetters, Norwich
and printed in Great Britain by Oxford University Press

# INTRODUCTION

When it became the turn of Maurice Barbanell – or Barbie as his friends always called him – to pass into the inner worlds, it was confidently expected that he would return to endorse at first hand the many other accounts which have reached us of life in the astral world. As a medium himself, and a life-long student of the subject, it was natural to expect him rapidly to become at home in his new environment, helped by an even closer rapport with his teacher, Silver Birch. One or two of his friends were confident he would swiftly pass to a high realm earned by his earth work.

But from his own account recorded in this book, these things did not happen as expected. At first he found considerable difficulty in identifying what was real in his environment and what only subjective to himself or illusory. Later, he found himself dividing his former Spiritualist peers into two groups, those who accepted the appearances around them and were content to live on without questioning them, and the others, like Barbie himself, who found exploration urgent and necessary if he was to grasp the meaning of what he was undergoing, and enlarging his own being by doing so. It is this uncomfortable and challenging process that he largely speaks about.

The account is made up of two loosely overlapping

1

parts. In the earlier passages Barbie relates his experiences at the time he was actually undergoing them, when they were by no means fully intelligible to him. In the later part, he looks back and attempts an orderly account of the process as he sees it now. Thus an element of repetition cannot altogether be avoided. It is necessary to bear in mind the different levels between the earlier and the later, deeper parts.

The references to the Old Fellow, the Old Man, the Old Chap, and the Old Gentleman, mostly refer to the teacher who bore the mask of Silver Birch when working with Barbie on earth, but who said then: 'I am not a Red Indian, I belong to another race in another part of the world that goes back much further.' Once or twice these names are used when Barbie is referring to the guide of another well-known medium.

There was an agreement between Barbie and myself that whoever died first would try to describe the true nature of experiences met with subsequently. This remains the main purpose rather than to provide personal factual evidence, though Barbie has referred at times to friends, peers, and others on earth, or encountered afterwards. Some of these brief references have been omitted, in order to allow the main narrative to stand out more clearly. Some I have included concern his best friend on earth and are somewhat intimate in content, and I am grateful to this friend for permission to include them.

Some readers, incidentally, may be inclined to scoff at an early reference, by way of light relief, to Hannen Swaffer's cigarette ash, reminiscent of the oft-quoted and misunderstood references to cigars in Oliver Lodge's *Raymond*, in that context, as in this, clearly a subjective creation and said by Raymond to be so.

Included as an interlude is a special Christmas sitting

2

when Barbie brought Estelle Roberts and Ena Twigg to greet me – two mediums to whom I owe a lot, and whose remarks seem to me characteristic. In an appendix Estelle brings a prominent Churchman, a man of evident integrity, if somewhat restricted, who wished to dissuade me from publishing this book, and who will be recognised as the one who formerly suppressed the Church report on Spiritualism.

In the main narrative Barbie shows himself to be a truthful witness, even when speaking to his own disadvantage. Inner events are shown as more important than outer ones, especially in experiences contrary to expectation. The interest in the second half of the book lies primarily in Barbie's inner life as a spiritual being. What he says strikes on the heart, and is clearly expressed in deep sincerity. Humility is seen to be a very genuine part of his character, though not likely to have been especially attributed to him formerly by those who only knew the outer Barbie, the journalist and editor.

Incidentally, there are amusing examples of editorial practices in these scripts, subjecting his medium to an occasional mild blue-pencilling, correcting an adjective into an adverb, and reproving her for starting sentences with 'He says'. 'Leave that out,' Barbie instructs her, 'just give my own words.'

It so happens that Marie Cherrie never met Barbie. She began these sessions with a certain resentment towards him, because in her view he had not given her an encouraging press as a young medium, nor had sufficiently supported her struggle to obtain better conditions for mediums. Nevertheless she put her private feelings aside and gave her fullest professional gifts to the task on all occasions. As Barbie says of her, reluctance was not resistance. It can fairly be said that with time a relationship of friendly respect has grown up between

3

them, and certainly one of full co-operation. Barbie did not at first consider Marie would be able to reproduce his own full vocabulary, so he chose a simplified form in which to express his ideas. Marie, skilled and self-effacing in establishing as accurate a dialogue as possible, recognises that some mistakes are inevitable. She refers to these as 'like missing a tennis ball'. Well, Becker misses a number in every match. For instance Marie Cherrie refers to Harry – apparently meaning Harry Edwards – where Barbie on earth would have called him Henry.

A noticeable feature is that whilst Barbie naturally hoped that Silver Birch would greet him on his arrival, he did not do so, although Barbie found later that he had been present behind the scenes. It was something of a shock too to find later on that their relationship was now less close; as he says, the partnership, like a business one, was now dissolved. This needed an important readjustment. He found too considerable problems in establishing where lay the realities of his new condition. He tells of areas which contain traps if they are persisted in for too long. He also found himself left much more to his own devices than is usually supposed, and as will be seen teachers gave him help sparsely and only when a particular need existed.

It will be noted that when Barbie first saw Silver Birch, it was in the form familiar from the portrait painted by Marcel Poncin. Yet Barbie suspected that he himself by prior expectation could be imposing this familiar image upon him. Later in what in apparent contradiction is again said to be the first time, he sees his guide in a form closer to his real self, and is obliged to enter into a much altered relationship with him.

The messages span a period of some four years. It might be considered that there has been ample time for Barbie to make all the adjustments needed. Not so. His

4

picture of what he has really found (or chose) is best judged by its own interior coherence, and by the sense of real experience it conveys, not least when Barbie finds himself perplexed, and at times confused by what is happening to him. He shows that life beyond death, as on earth, is far from simple. He is clearly very much still earning his living, not of course in terms of money, but in terms of growth in consciousness.

Above all, as the result of new experiences and new value judgments, Barbie has himself changed in some respects. What would his account be worth if it does not show such change? Any assessment needs to take note of these and to understand them as far as possible.

Barbie himself is well aware of the limitations of evidence in general. Some of his friends, he says, will accept this account, others will say it is not him. He adds that on earth he too would have doubted, much as they do.

If these doubters are right in their estimate, their task is not done in merely leaving the matter there. If this is not Barbie, and personally I certainly believe he is the communicator, it is possible for a sceptic to say in an easy way that the whole of the material could be drawn from the store of memories of those who knew him. However nobody has ever been able to put forward an explanation of how such super-ESP can be achieved, nor would such a joint production at all account for the clear and largely unwavering personal purpose evident throughout. Where else lies the source of the self-criticisms and regrets expressed? The sceptic must be asked too to come forward with a view of who the speaker is, if not Barbie, and how he has been able to enter into so much of Barbie's mind.

Very many communicators have said they have found the process to be far more difficult than they had expected it to be. It is necessary and only fair to respect the difficulties a medium also has to overcome. She has first to grasp ideas, unfamiliar and perhaps alien to her, and then to express them as best she can in accordance with the communicator's intention, but inevitably partly coloured in reception by her own concepts. In the early days Marie said, 'I hear his thoughts, but not in actual words.' Thus she was obliged partly to rely on her own vocabulary. A critic is on dangerous ground in demanding too close a replica of what Barbie might have said on earth, and of the words he would have been likely to choose. Certainly some old characteristics and foibles and perhaps some tightly-held views and prejudices will be likely to rub off onto what the medium is able to transmit. But these are Barbie's less important parts. The further our communicators penetrate into the inner worlds, then as they so often say, the harder it is to describe, and the fainter becomes the pattern of their earth personality – and the fainter their interest in it too.

We cannot say what Barbie 'ought' to experience, for if communication is to develop in a significant way, departures must be expected from old and sometimes simplistic or heavily larded accounts. If this is not so, it would mean that the subject can be closed on the grounds that there is nothing more to learn. But if one thing is certain about discarnate communication, it is that it is both limited and incomplete in expression, and to overcome this, a growth of depth is required in recipients also, if they are to understand new things which teachers are beginning to expound. Barbie shows us something of his own changes, and how he finds he is able to confront further new situations only as a result of such changes already brought about in and by himself. He is gradually being transformed, and is transforming himself; the two go together.

6

# INTRODUCTION

There had been times on earth, as is correctly said, when Barbie and I had little to say to one another. Indeed our ideas continued to be opposed in a number of ways. As a friend I came to value his warmth, to appreciate his frequent actions to put his own teachings into practice, and the dedication which I came to understand more and more clearly. Since his death, and as a result of the story told in these pages, our friendship has become deeper, and my respect and affection for him has grown. I look forward to renewing this friendship face to face in due course.

Paul Beard

PART I

In this three-way conversation Maurice Barbanell's comments are in ordinary roman type, Paul Beard's are in italic, and Marie Cherrie's are prefixed with §. However where Mrs Cherrie interrupts Barbanell her comments are in square brackets.

ONE

## 24TH FEBRUARY 1982

§ Now I don't know what the relevance of this is but there's a man's voice quoting from a hymn book – 'You in your small corner and me in mine.' He also says we've had some conflicts in the past and this would be you and him he's speaking of.

*Yes – quite correct if it's who I think it is.*

§ You didn't always agree and I would imagine in the conflict at times where this man was concerned with you there would be no holds barred, not politeness, but really seeing things from a different angle and yet he said, 'We worked for the same people.'

*That's right.*

§ He is saying we're both scribblers, both scribblers, I think he means writers and he's laughing, he says, 'You still sit there weighing things up.' You must have done this sometimes in his company too when he was here. A very forceful man. I would imagine this man could be dogmatic by the force of his thoughts, you know. I say I hear them, I do hear them but not in actual words. But his words, his thoughts are forceful. I would imagine this man would not suffer fools gladly.

It is a bit of a blow when you come over here and you

11

look back at your life and you can see it objectively. I did expect this but I don't think I realised what it would reveal. It seems at times as if I acted in such a way that the ends justified the means.

§ Somehow this disturbs him, as if then he could rationalise and explain away certain things he did here but he can't now. It's something to do with work he did here, as if he's been a bit disillusioned now, that he thought that his motives were good and he's seeing them a little bit differently. He says it's a strange thing, this reality. You've got to realise constantly that you'll only see what you want to see and so you've to make a conscious effort to broaden the field and sometimes you're seduced by seeing what you want to see. He still won't let me see his face. He stands in the shadow. I wouldn't call him a tall man, you understand, although he would give an impression of height. I know his passing was quick.

*Yes.*

§ I know also that he was well prepared for it, had in fact put into action certain things for such an event. He's talking about a protégé of his who seems to be carrying on some work for him and he says he's pleased and yet you know I get the feeling that this man would not give up the reins lightly, he is not someone who would find it easy to delegate.

*This is correct.*

§ He gave these reins to his protégé but I get the feeling that if he had a chance he'd snatch them back, as if 'No, not that way' and yet when I asked him if this protégé was doing well he said 'Yes, but he's going to find his hands tied in many ways'. There seem to be a group of people who tie him, limit him and yet I know that the communicator had a hand in this, you know; in other words giving them the reins but also controlling them. Yes. He's talking about a wife. I don't know if he says he's worried about his wife or he has been worried about her.

*I understand the reference.*

§ He says she's doing well but her strength isn't all it should be. He is also laughing and saying something about animals. I don't know if she loves animals or she has animals but he's saying something about animals. There must be a link with his wife.

*That's quite correct.*

§ I don't know if you and this man ever sat in a sort of committee or anything together . . .

*Yes, we did.*

§ . . . he defeated you; I feel it was to do with voting power or casting a vote. He says, 'I'm not sure that my way was the right way but I felt it was the only way it could work. I felt it was the only way.'

I don't know if he had doubts at the time but I would suspect he's got doubts now because he sounds apologetic.

*Tell him no need to apologise.*

§ He felt it was the only way the thing could take off. 'Tell him,' he says, 'I'm always seeing myself as a bit of a showman, a salesman and all that that implies regarding the public.

'Tell him I've met the dear Vicar over here.'

*I wonder which dear Vicar he means?*

13

§ The one we both knew very well and he's saying something about weather . . .

*I think I know who he means.*

§ Weather . . .

*Go on – you're doing very well. It's not finished but I can understand it.*

§ And he's saying something about Leslie I think.

*What's he found in the dear Vicar then?*

§ Some contentment, some frustration, in fact quite a lot of frustration. 'I got a bit of a lecture,' he's laughing, and I'm getting a picture of a finger wagging.

Do you know, one thing I notice about my communicator is his shining shoes; it's the only thing I can see clearly. Was he very particular about his shoes because I keep seeing these black shiny shoes?

*They would always be very clean.*

§ Because it is the only part of him I can see, just his shoes and oh sorry – and a hand with a ring on it, quite a heavy ring. Because I only got a glimpse of that. He must have worn spectacles because he says he doesn't need to look for them any more. Now whether he was in the habit of misplacing them, or not, I don't know. He's talking about a Trust that has been set up and he seems to have some doubts about it. I get this doubting feeling from him and yet he's not against it but there are doubts there.

*Now this could apply to one of two Trusts and I don't know whether he could identify which he is referring to. It's a bit hard I know.*

§ Both. He says he knows human nature. This man

could be cynical at times because the way he said it was a little bit cynical. As if he wouldn't have any illusions or fool himself. Yes, both trusts, but there's one you're more interested in and one he's more interested in. Don't say that you haven't had your doubts because you have.

*Yes.*

§ Especially over the last period – I'm going back into last year. The doubts have always been a little bit there but they've become stronger. And he's giving me an expression which is familiar to me, he's saying too many chiefs and not enough Indians. Too many supervising and not enough working. He is aware that he is on a rather low level at the moment and therefore a lot of what he would tell you, you would already know at this level. He's amazed at the number of people who have been over here for some time and who show no inclination to learn or become more aware. He will take every advantage of moving on, when he feels that certain things that still link him here are all settled. He speaks again of worry over wife, helping her to get her balance. There's a lot of energy from this man, restless energy, but it's not so much physical as mental. I know that a couple of times when I've been a bit slow in picking him up he's become a little bit ratty, but then this is back to not suffering fools gladly.

He says, 'You'll hear from me', and then just as he was leaving he said, 'There is no death'. Then he laughed and said, 'You will live after you die' and as I feel him fade away he just said it was better this time.

*Oh, the communication?*

§ Yes, I've got that impression and he seemed satisfied although I would say he is not an easy man to be satisfied.

15

## TWO

## 18TH JANUARY 1984

It's much more exciting than I expected, the possibilities are endless and quite daunting. Still some confusion with realities, so much depends on what you want to see. Difficult to keep readjusting. Mother's reality is not my reality.

*I see.*

When I am with her have to accept her reality.

*Because she would not be able to accept yours quite so readily?*

Wouldn't understand it, confuse her. Understand the experience of seeing through their eyes. Like speaking to people with different points of view, only the points of view are reflected around them. And so they have reality. Can be confusing. I am groping towards my own reality, can't be sure if I have achieved it yet. I know how easy it is to see what you expect to see. Must be careful to stay away from this trap. Comfortable trap but still a trap. Guide says I'm on my own now. Get a little bit of help but not a lot. Tremendous sense of well-being, feel you could move mountains. Probably could if you knew how! Hear people's thoughts as if they are speaking.

*Could be disconcerting.*

Some very uncontrolled. First thing I've learned – to discipline my thoughts, not always remember however.

*Has he met Myers?*

No, hope to. Possibility that his awareness is beyond mine.

*Yes, understood.*

Apart from certain people I still care about, I am not really interested in anything else on this level. Too much to learn, understand over here. Need a lot of will-power and discipline over myself. Concentration not always easy.

*Why is this?*

On your level don't need to concentrate all the time, only for periods. Over here concentration needed. Think it's because I'm still a beginner.

*What happens if your concentration fails over there?*

Other people's reality intrudes.

*I see, I understand.*

Become confused. Probably haven't worked it out properly yet. Even doing this, can't afford to let attention wander, else confusion of thoughts confuses medium. Think of keeping your thoughts disciplined all the time.

*Not an easy thing to consider.*

Only way if you want to move on. Using muscles which haven't been used before, muscles of discipline, will-power. Always thought I was good at concentrating. Realise periods of concentration, but not concentrating all the time. Still think I might be getting it wrong. Maybe there's an easier way. Notice others who have been here longer not having same difficulty.

17

*Maybe this is partly because you're still a medium in a way and so pick up things very easily, other people's thoughts, other people's pictures of reality?*

Part of this possible. Didn't realise how undisciplined I was in my thinking.

*Aren't we all?*

Have been trying to evaluate knowledge – difficult. Balancing the ledgers. Try not to rationalise. Spent periods of time angry with myself. Tried to turn mistakes into learning periods sometimes, but in all honesty not always. Must not lie to myself, no advantage – disadvantage. Didn't realise how much I would miss not having set of rules. Didn't realise freedom would be so difficult.

Lower life forms seem to return, not clear on this yet. Had my own opinion about this before I came over.

*Do you mean return as themselves or return as part of the pool?*

Part of the pool. Not sure but think some people too. Haven't discovered exact knowledge about this yet but looks like it. We've discussed this in the past. We disagreed. Will tell you more when I've found out. Seem to be periods when I rest, can't call it sleep.

*Are they thought-filled or are they empty, these periods?*

Seem to turn inward during those periods.

*Yes, like a reverie.*

Yes, don't know how long they last. Light everywhere without a particular source. Not sure if this is reality. Got to be careful, if successful might be creating other reality, seems to be so.

*You mean a private reality or part of the big reality?*

Private reality.

*So it would have a temporary life period, private reality?*

Yes. Sometimes in trying to be aware of permanent reality you can fool yourself by creating your own reality. No good checking with others. The people I know over here have similar thoughts to me, therefore realities might match.

Only help we get is from higher sources, but they are not always with us. Even then given things to think about rather than told direct. Terrible temptation to stop striving, it can be so comfortable. Still you know me well enough to know I must keep looking round next corner.

*Yes indeed.*

Find I have to be here to speak to you.

*You have to be here? You mean come down to this level?*

Yes but more *surroundings*.

*You mean you're aware of the building or the room?*

Yes.

*Surprising.*

No, I know I don't need to do it but can't quite get used to it yet.

*I see.*

Habit I think.

*Yes.*

Tried to imagine the telephone. Thought if I was going to do that I might as well come. If I have to physically imagine one thing I might as well do the rest.

*Yes I understand.*

No difference. Will tell you when I have conquered this. Must admit, lot of your stuff fits in. [§ And now he's laughing and saying, 'But try and live it, not so easy.']

19

*No indeed.*

Quite a lot of people over here have life so similar to what they've left, hardly any difference. My relatives wonder what I'm up to.

*I can believe that!*

Ask me why do I do everything the difficult way. Don't intend to go too far ahead, must help Sylvia but can learn the beginnings. Passing itself was easy, like going into another room, best description. Like going to sleep and waking up. Was aware of tunnel effect, saw relatives. Next period a bit of a blur. Think I was resting, can't remember much. Periods of awareness but not all aware. Remember communicating with you.

*Yes.*

And a few others but that period very dreamlike, not like now.

*What about the old gang on his side? Which does he feel closest to there at the moment?*

§ He says there's more over there than there are here on earth. Estelle; Harry; the other Harry although we still argue; Hannen – we also argue – Jack.

*Jack the materialiser?*

Yes. Phyllis.

*Phyllis? Who would that be?*

You wouldn't have known her. Long time ago.

*I see.*

Helen. [§ He says medium.]

*Yes. Helen H.*

Leslie.

*Leslie?*

It's a man.

*Yes, I wonder which one?*

§ Talks about meeting him briefly.

*Does he mean the one who wagged his finger at him?*

Yes. [§ I don't feel they would be close.]

*No, I wouldn't suppose so either.*

Like a conventional meeting, not real closeness.

*Some time would you like to give me some sort of message for the Saturday afternoon lot?*

Yes. Tell them maybe they'll listen to me more, though knowing that crowd they still won't!

*I don't think they will. Can't you shake them up in some way?*

I'll try.

*Right. That would be fun. You've been talking about just the things that were interesting me. Some time in this series maybe you'd like to say something about the future of the Movement as you see it. You see I'm thinking of you as a sort of hypodermic syringe here and there.*

Perfect. Just what I would like to be. Will do my best.

*Good, You've done very well today.*

Medium letting me speak more. Must go.

*Delighted to talk to you. All the old comradeship is there you know.*

I know. Peace be with you.

*Thank you.*

§ One of Silver Birch's expressions. Now he's gone.

21

## THREE

## 1st FEBRUARY 1984

§ He still has some interest in where the Movement's heading. He says it's difficult. Part of him sees that side of his life as over, that side of his growth, part of him still maintains some interest. He says he's aware that there are many people over here trying to get certain truths through in many different ways.

*Does he mean more on the philosophical side?*

§ Yes. And not only in the Movement. Anywhere there is awareness, spiritual growth, not just inside the Movement. He says there has been concern on his part, more when he was on earth, but still there is some concern now, that the Movement has been becoming like other religious organisations.

*Yes.*

§ 'We used to talk of this. You felt the Christian Church wouldn't do much harm to it. I felt it could do.' Your fears were not as great as his regarding the Movement either standing still and becoming very hidebound, or being taken over by Christianity, the Church, he means.

*The latter didn't worry me because it seemed so unlikely.*

§ That's what he says, 'It was more a fear to me than

to you. I still have this fear and being in the spirit world hasn't changed this fear. I have always realised that there are people who need to hedge themselves round with rules, you could almost say with dogma. A spirit that is free thinking and questing is not easy for some people to take and understand. They feel a certain security where there is a book of rules or modes of conduct to follow. You've given me quite a headache trying to formulate what I would say to you. I have also tried to get the opinion of others here.'

*Good.*

Some of my medium friends have helped me, some are prejudiced, yet as you know some of them were among the first pioneers and all were individualists, not tied to any rules. As one said to me we made the rules up as we went along, we were discovering them. [§ He's talking about speaking with Arthur. 'Arthur's disappointed,' he says.]

*Arthur from Scotland?*

Yes. Not gone the way planned.

*Or perhaps the plan was wrong?*

No criteria, not enough teaching. Hannen just argues, he had strong feelings. Harry looks to science and says science has been dragging its feet. He's annoyed with the book they have brought out to do with him.

*Oh why?*

Saying that he didn't conduct experiments right, properly. He said the authors, not author, authors, can't make their mind up whether he's a fool or a charlatan. Harry always more interested in the individual than the group effort. Didn't work well in groups, with groups.

One good sign – over here I am more aware of many

more people becoming interested in the unseen world. More people looking, but standard is bad, never known it to be so low. Ironic. More people looking now than before, yet past standard higher. Often wonder how many would be around if we were still illegal. Many attracted by the publicity.

*Yes.*

Certainly have been told world moving into more spiritual awareness. Problem: who is to teach? Squabbles, arguments. No united effort, no help from Churches Fellowship, get more help from the scientists. See it all falling apart before it is reassembled.

*I see. That wouldn't surprise me.*

Only way. Foundations too weak to build on, must make new ones. Sounds as if I'm advocating old ways best. No! Values are wrong now, they form a weak foundation. Not just my opinion, others too.

*Yes.*

Confirmed. Realise value of publicity, important, publicity, but narrow tightrope, very easy to get wrong publicity, handled wrongly. No need to challenge Churches, not much power there any more, will find some attempt to join us in effort to regain standing. Told over here two more Popes, no more. After this one, two. Haven't explained why. I'm not that good at looking far ahead yet, others told me this. Can't give reason, they did not give me one. Don't know if this is to do with Church falling or some other event.

*Maybe they're not allowed to say?*

You learn over here not to question until you know right questions.

*That's wisdom.*

Guide sends regards.

*Thank you.*

Don't see him much, now and again. There was a time when there was a friendly argument.

§ This friendly argument seems to have been linked with his guide. I don't know if it was something you were involved in or witness to. He says you were all pleased when guide made questioner end up answering own question. 'Five of us there that evening,' not including me,' he says, 'three now in spirit, including me.'

Was going to give you a speech.

*Well, very good, you've made plenty.*

May do so before our experiment finished with. But decided to let you write this one up your own way if you want to use it.

*Maybe this will just break up the ground a bit.*

Am moving slowly. Having at the moment to sort out my vanities, not easy.

*I should have thought those would have punctured themselves.*

Some remain, some difficult to get rid of, rationalise them. Vanities to do with reason for doing things here, vanities to do with real soul growth and posturing, must understand weaknesses, not hide behind excuses or what seems to be good reason.
My old colleague still smoking, even over here.

*Really?*

25

Filthy habit. Ash down his front. You'll remember him like this.

*I remember him smoking alright, yes indeed.*

But he's showing me the bottom of a suit that would have ash on it, as if it would spill.

*No this I wouldn't remember.*

Or sometimes be forgotten about, you understand?

*Yes I understand.*

Think he only does it to shock and be an individualist. This is in character with the man.

*Yes.*

Find that I can know when you're coming by reading your thoughts.

*Ah, well I sent you out a thought or two this morning.*

Picked it up. First wasn't sure if I was going to get the time right, visions of turning up at wrong time. Silly, easy when you know how. Still feel need to come down to this level.

*Whilst communicating?*

Yes. Know I shouldn't need to but doesn't feel comfortable, feel I want to shout.

*If you could do it by not coming down so far, would there be more of you available so to speak? Mentally?*

Think so. Found it easier to give a speech when I was on earth. Working through third party not so easy, depends on degree of penetration. Think I could be successful, need more time.

26

FOUR

## 22ND FEBRUARY 1984

§ He's still having trouble with time. It seems very little time has passed since he last spoke, yet knowing you as he does, he says, 'You're very organised, so I presume a certain amount of time has elapsed.'

*Yes but not too much, only a fortnight.*

I continue to find difficulty in controlling my thoughts. I would have said of myself that I was disciplined in this way when I was in this world.

*I would have said so too.*

But compared with over here I realise I was only a beginner. I can sustain it for periods and these periods are getting longer but there are also periods when I cannot remember what I have done or where I have been.

*Do you mean on earth or over there?*

Over here. One could almost call them blackouts.

*Can they be recovered later on?*

So I have been told. I have been told by others that my time sense and awareness will get better but I was never a patient man. I have been told that I am trying to learn things too quickly.

27

*Well that's no fault.*

To run before I can walk! – but, as you know, this will not put me off. At first I found the periods of blackout annoying, now I find them intriguing. Almost as if my awareness comes in fits and starts. I have a theory it is caused because of the sustained concentration and that I am still adjusting and have not always made allowances for this. Others say that this wears off in time. I feel content in myself enough, there is no mental discomfort, a sense of well-being is more or less constant with me but I am also conscious of an urge to learn as much as possible. Like feeling hungry but you don't know what you're hungry for. I find that I have increasingly to concentrate to be interested in what is happening on your level.

*Doesn't belong to you any more?*

At times it seems very dream-like. It seems to need an effort of will to concentrate on. These periods when I speak to you encourage this.

*Are they tiresome to you in a way?*

They start off that way, then I become interested.

*I see.*

And of course there are still ties of love where I remain interested in the well-being of those close to me. I have tried to analyse this. It is possible that because I have such an enquiring mind I have pulled more away from the bonds than the average person whose sole interests were family and friends. This is a possibility. But we spend so much of our time on this level speculating on the nature of things and what could be learned, to us this is a great adventure to be explored as much as possible. This may be why we did not hear so much from the brilliant minds

28

of previous centuries, for by the very nature of their thinking they would have been drawn further away from the level they had left.

*Yes, understood.*

This may also explain why the average person has less trouble contacting relatives, again and again, for they merely continue to do what they did on earth. One thing you become aware of over here is that although there can be some help and guidance given by others most of the progress is done by you. There is a sense of *déjà vu* about the whole thing. One is constantly coming up against an inner knowledge, an inner knowing that recognises and understands what is taking place.

*So this is both old memories and a condition to which you will restore yourself?*

Yes. One of my first recollections when I passed over was to rid myself of a dream-like feeling. I can see now why it would be so easy for people to exist in this state and find it difficult to come out of it. Unless one were aware of this and prepared for it, one could exist in this state for some time. Being prepared for it, I was on my guard and was not seduced by it. We were right, however, transition is easy. I suppose I had to prove it for myself. It is all very well to be told this but to experience it gives you personal proof. I am aware of some conflict between my friends since I left.

*You mean between themselves or about you?*

About me. I cannot blame them for this because if I was in your world I too would be taking part in this.

*Tell me about this conflict.*

They are not sure I'm communicating. I do not blame

29

them for this. Many times in the past I too doubted when others communicated but now the shoe is on the other foot, I realise the problems others who came before me had in coming out with irrefutable evidence. I have been thinking, trying to come up with something that would remove the doubts but looking at each of them it would take not the one piece of evidence to remove their doubts, but individual evidence for each of them. I can only continue as I have been doing and hope over the period slowly to pile up the evidence of my return. One of the things that has been complained of is the form of speech that I am now using but I am trying to keep what I am saying in simple form.

*The more laconic the better I feel.*

For if I were to revert completely to my old speech pattern and verbal usage there would be always the danger of misinterpretation. If I keep the words simple then there cannot be so many meanings taken from them. Tell my chief disbeliever I was with him recently and he was aware of my presence. Tell him I tried to make a noise that he would hear and to move an object but I'm not very good at that yet. I was only able to move it a little bit but it was on his desk. Tell him I was also aware of some old notes he was reading through recently. Tell him he should have them in better order. Tell him I have fully expected him to react in this manner and that I am glad he's sticking true to type. [§ He is showing me something that looks like a heavy inkwell or paperweight that would be linked with this man, but it's something heavy that would be on the desk.]

*That's what he tried to move?*

§ Yes. He's laughing, he says, 'It's never been my way to do things the easy way. Maybe if I'd tried for something lighter I would have had more success.'

*Perhaps you could turn a page over on his desk?*

§ Yes he says he has thought of that. One thing it has brought home to him is how difficult it is to convince and as someone who in the past needed a lot of convincing, he is being paid back in kind!

I saw our old friend Lang.

*Do you mean Lang of the Church report?*

Yes.

You won't be surprised to hear that he hasn't made a tremendous amount of progress.

*Did he shake you by the left hand?*

He realises the harm he aided, but he says he harmed himself more in the long run.

*Yes.*

Even with the knowledge he now has there is still a narrowness of vision there and I found him a very self-centred sort. His thoughts seem to turn constantly inwards instead of outwards, inwards to his own problems. It seems to me that he thinks his spiritual knowledge should have achieved a better level for him and this is something he is still having difficulty coming to terms with.

*Perhaps Dick Sheppard would help him.*

Dick – says he's tried but the man is hidebound, blinkered, although not as bad as he was. Dick is very much his usual self.

*Good, and what a lovely self that was.*

31

Still as cheerful as ever. Get the feeling he isn't telling me everything, keeps saying you'll understand that later, old chap, when I ask him. Feel as if I'm back at school again.

*Your best friend, Tony, finds it difficult to believe the communications because, as he puts it, you were a sophisticated soul, an old soul with many incarnations behind you with great knowledge of the subject, why are you hung up in these ways? He thinks you should just go straight through, slick.*

Tell him I wish I could. Tell him he has a higher idea of me than I have had. Tell him quarrel with word 'sophistication'. Tell him to look word up in dictionary, he will find that has no place over here. Tell him that although I have some awareness of previous lives still not clear.

*He meant that you'd been through death a number of times before so it should be easy in his view to get adjusted to it.*

No, because each time soul has different awareness. Think it's easier to pass when you're primitive, don't know what's happening, don't question; when more evolved, it's more complicated – not that it should be so. I came over with many questions, many things to do and learn, told you about *déjà vu.*

Simple native passing, doesn't question, accepts. More knowledge, more awareness, more problems. Becoming more familiar with level but not skimming straight through.

*This is where experience defeats logic doesn't it?*

Yes. More simple the soul, more acceptance. More soul evolves, more questions to be answered, more awareness and need to know and understand. Understand now why some guides speak in riddles; even explaining is difficult, different concepts at work.

32

## FIVE

## 29TH FEBRUARY 1984

§ He undertands you want to ask him questions about the lapses in consciousness, awareness.

*Yes. Now he mentioned a vague awareness of former lives. Has he memory of any former life that throws a light on why he had to do the job he did this time?*

§ 'Glimmers,' he says, 'glimmers.' He knows that he had to come back to do what he did because of religious intolerance.

*He means his own in a former time?*

§ Yes. That now he had to stick with truth without the trappings of religion. He thinks this is why he was so anti-religion when he was here this time round.

I was so aware on a subconscious level that I was not to be trapped again in this vicious circle. I'm not sure if I held a position officially in a religious body but these are part of the glimmers that I have picked up since I came over.

*It makes sense doesn't it?*

But I know I have the feeling quite strongly that although I didn't do it all right I did not do too badly this time round.

33

*Did this feeling come from yourself, or were you told it by your guide?*

From myself. It's a strange feeling. I've had something similar here in your world where you feel you've done something right yet you're not sure what exactly it is you've done. You've had it too. A feeling of being pleased, yet something you can't put your finger on.

*Do you feel a bigger person now than you felt yourself to be on earth?*

I feel closer to the knowledge I want, but no, I haven't noticed any change in that direction.

*How will you get this thirst for knowledge satisfied where you are?*

I don't know, I'm feeling my way at the moment.

*Would you say these halls of learning we so often hear about are symbols really or do you think they're actual buildings of some fine material?*

Can be buildings, but only for those who want them as buildings.

*I see. Have you met some old clergymen friends/enemies who now realise that they've got guides to learn from?*

One or two.

*Have you met the Rev. Fingerwag again?*

No, not yet. Find that people that come over here with prejudices are not easy to speak with. Seem to exist in a world of their own. Talking about someone called Pike. Pike's O.K.

*Well Bishop Pike never was too tight in the fetters was he?*

34

No and much looser now. Good man. Calls himself a missionary over here.

My awareness increasing but still have problems with time. Haven't lost my temper.

*Well one didn't see it very often but one knew it was there.*

Haven't got an audience the way I used to have on earth. Know I'm not starting from scratch but feel sometimes I am. Find that you gravitate towards certain type of people here.

*What sort of type?*

People on the same level, bit like on earth. Exchange thoughts and ideas, help each other understand. Don't have much contact with guides yet, seem to be busy with their own business.

*Is that because you relied a bit too much when you were here?*

Think so. Feel that this part I've got to do by myself.

*Yes. Well as you've got this sense of well-being, that's fine isn't it?*

Yes but you know my questions. I thought I would be rid of most of them when I came over, but I have a different lot now.

*You don't surprise me.*

Little group of us together over here.

*Is there a leader?*

Not yet but some over here longer than I. Really just exchanging thoughts, ideas. Two of them old friends. One of them a medium – three. One's Peter.

*Which Peter is that?*

Not in my line of work nor yours. [§ He seems to be giving me a link with Peter Sellers.]

*Peter Sellers? Oh really. Well it's not unlikely.*

§ Because he keeps showing me movies and theatres.

Clever man. Open mind. There is also a woman medium, old friend of ours, you know who.

*I think so.*

Others in group from different walks of life, not known before. Reminds me a bit of our old group, working out where we were to go from there. See other old friends but seem to end up working with this group.

*Expect you've got a bit of a mission there.*

Not sure, still trying to work it out. Meet up from time to time, discuss things over here but also lot of individual work, progress.

*Work on yourself you mean?*

Yes. Find family links not so important. I mean family links when in spirit, not on earth.

*Yes I see.*

Once seen, or after spending some time with them, it seems to be enough.

*No true affinity in fact?*

Yes. Discussed this with others. Peter had big thing about his mother. We've realised that if you're on the level of family links being important, then it tends to keep you there. Almost first real step you make over here, to meet and leave your family. Not permanently . . .

*But not cloistered with them?*

Yes. Realise there are groups of people over here who are still very much clinging to their families. No progress until they move beyond that. Some find this difficult to do. This is why it's a big step. Was lucky that I was only close to one or two. Maybe would have found it more difficult, if my emotional life with them had been different.

*You needed the freedom I expect?*

Yes. Find that to continue on their level holds one back, going over old ground again and again.

Nothing achieved. Peter found this too. Too clever a mind to stay at that level, even though attachment was strong. These kinds of things we talk over as a group, understanding, helping, pointing out what weve noticed individually, trying to understand it. I don't feel guilty about this.

*No, why should you?*

§ 'Background.' Coming from his background, family ties were supposedly very strong.

*Yes, because of his race.*

§ Yes. This is why he mentions not feeling guilty, as if he should have felt guilty with the background he had.

Realise they are alright, know I am alright, no more needs. That part of life now fading into the past. Very eager to find out how things are when Sylvia joins. Think it will be alright.

*Pity she can't get released.*

Not yet. Also others here of old group, wonder if they'll fit in, wonder if they'll want to? Aware of how much is

37

hidden when you're on your level. Might have expected *our* man, but not Peter. You understand.

*Yes.*

Swaff goes his own way. Says he'll work it out himself, always was a loner. Enjoy talking to him. Seems to take opposite angle still.

*Is that deliberate?*

Yes. Devil's Advocate. [§ He is speaking as if this was a nickname for him. Saying to me he wouldn't have used it before because I wouldn't have passed it on. He didn't feel he could trust me with the nickname, I would have thought I was mishearing.

*Oh I think he might have ventured.*

§ No. He says, play cautious. More likelihood of other name being accepted.

*Yes.*

Can't tell you how long spent with group, this kind of thing difficult but know there are periods we're together.

SIX

## 17TH AUGUST 1984

§ I'm aware of the one who called himself Maurice Barbanell standing beside you. I never saw this man in the flesh. Did he stoop a little bit, Paul?

*A little bit, yes.*

§ You know just a slight suggestion of round shoulders.

*Round shoulders because he was writing at his desk all day long.*

Am clearer in my mind now.

*Good.*

Was like walking around in a fog, almost like trying to stop myself day dreaming, best description I can give. Took quite a bit of effort at first to do this.

*But you reckon you're clear now?*

Almost. Like waking up but dream still lingers. Have to shake myself awake, to get rid of it.

Keep reminding my old staff because I'm not there to do it any more. Have to slow my thoughts down to communicate this way, very painstaking. Never realised the faster level till I came back. Can explain why last sitting wasn't successful. Medium's health below par.

Always hit this problem with human instrument. Feel medium's energy level has a lot to do with it; it fluctuates. Maybe medium's health low at periods because of fluctuating energy levels.

*You mean the psychic fluctuations can upset the physical health?*

Yes. Maybe we've been putting the cart before the horse – the other way round. Not sure, but I'm thinking this. Thought I'd speak of this to see what you would think.

*It's hard to form a worth-while opinion about it, it's a point to notice and watch isn't it?*

§ He's nodding again and he's saying, 'We used to do this, bounce ideas off each other.' I can't get the words . . . 'I'll watch from my side, you watch from yours.' I have to mention here that he wears spectacles as I'm looking at him and he keeps pushing them up as if they're sliding down. Did he ever do this? Or was it maybe just a habit he had, because he keeps touching them. I have to say that. He says he's glad I noticed that mannerism, so it is a mannerism, he said he did it deliberately.

*Does he, in his ordinary way of living now, does he talk by telepathy or by words?*

Thought.

*Thought, yes.*

Find words clumsy now.

*Do you have a similar kind of difficulty in expressing via telepathy or does that disappear?*

Difficult, have to keep thoughts simple; with complex thoughts too much could go wrong.

40

*That's in your ordinary life now?*

No, in communication.

Depending on people you are with, complex or simple, much the same as on earth. Way you would talk to one person very plainly, simply, other more complex.

*Yes, but in both cases by thought, by telepathy?*

Yes.

*I never thought to find you without a word!*

Know the group is still not totally convinced I'm communicating. Some are, some are not but then I would be the same in their place. It will all have to be individual.

*I see and if they won't come to the water it's a difficult thing isn't it?*

You know, I know, that what convinces you will not convince them and vice versa. Although they treat this in a scientific way there will still be that need for personal evidence, something that will be relative between myself and them. Have spent some time travelling.

*Up or down?*

Wish I could go up! Little bit down, not much, more across.

*Is it more different than you expected?*

In some ways it's familiar to me, like an echo.

*After all, you've done it before.*

But in other ways different. Think it's because I'm more aware this time. Maybe awareness makes the difference. Amazing the number of people who live in their own worlds, can't reach them.

41

*Are you talking about intellectuals chiefly?*

Not always.

*What about parsons?*

Yes this applies to them. You talk on your level about people living in a world of their own. More so here. [§ He keeps correcting my grammar!] Everyone jumps on the band waggon. Original truth's gone.

*Are we not asking enough of our mediums?*

You're not asking enough. Not enough discipline. Work harder.

*It's the leisure that I feel is important.*

Yes. Right idea. It was the right idea that there should be a stipend. Difficult to work out how to do it.

*Yes, very.*

Yet it would be the answer to the problem. Didn't always think this way but do more now. Exclusive use. Abused by trivia. Maybe can be got round by different levels.

§ I asked him why he doesn't give me all the names, he says he doesn't want me distracted. He says – yes I understand – he says I might know bits and pieces about certain people without realising it and so he'd rather talk without that.

*Yes. I think he's right don't you?*

§ Yes but it's irritating. He says he doesn't want me speculating and then adding bits. He says he wouldn't let his writers get away with it, his reporters, and he won't let me get away with it, adding bits, do you understand?

*Yes.*

Have watched communication taking place with this medium, guide and people who come forward. I was right, the guide gives them instructions. Remember we spoke of this? Some of them too hesitant.

*Yes. Are they able to have a kind of re-run afterwards to see how well they got on or has it all gone?*

It's all gone. Some are in a quite emotional state, quite emotional.

*Pity you can't record it all on your side.*

They could if they knew how to do it.

*You mean it's not impossible?*

There is no time. They could go back through the experience again but they don't understand this.

*You mean it's written in their memory somewhere?*

No, not written in their memory, written in the vibrations. [§ No I know I'm not getting it right what he's saying.] It's like re-playing a video, could you understand that? You don't need to remember something, you can re-play it, have a re-play of it.

*So are you saying that in thought terms it's the equivalent of putting it on a video?*

Only you're actually experiencing the whole thing again. [§ I don't know if I've explained that as well as he wanted to. It's difficult to explain.]

*Yes. Ask him if it is like Mrs Willett recalling her childhood and being it again?*

Yes and so then you can learn.

43

*Does he want to come back to me less often or more often?*

More often, more work.

*Right. We'll gradually work out some sort of system perhaps?*

Yes. Now fog's clearing, will be easier. Will only come when I feel instrument strong enough.

## SEVEN

## 21ST SEPTEMBER 1984

*Can I know how much you relate to Silver Birch these days?*

Getting one's bearings is the difficulty. It's so easy to wander off in tangents. Sometimes I feel I was closer to Silver Birch when I was on earth.

*Why is that?*

We worked together.

*Yes, I understand.*

It's as if he's left me to find my own way now. Like partners dissolving a business and going on to do their own work. I'm with him sometimes, usually for a lecture.

*What does he look like now in comparison with the portrait?*

Very similar but thinner, thinner than I expected. The trouble is I never know if he's showing me himself as I expect to see him or if this is truly how he looks, or looked. Not that there is ever a wish to deceive but awareness is difficult, you miss the nuances.

*I would have thought the nuances would be easier to pick up.*

Over here you become more conscious of how your

thoughts direct your awareness. I see him as I expect to see him but am unsure if this is my reality.

*I think I take the point.*

The last time I was with him, he spoke of the difficulty of being distracted. From what I gather, this distraction can be caused by being caught up in another's reality. I have been exploring the level I find myself on and he warned that in this exploration I could become confused unless my own sense of reality is strong.

*Like going into a Catholic or a Jewish family and finding yourself adopting their ideas?*

Or being with someone over a period of time and finding out that you're picking up their accent if they have a strong one. Same sort of thing. Only not so easy to be aware of.

*You've spoken of this difficulty several times so it must be a very real one.*

Yes. Keep wanting to see what lies ahead. He has told me I wouldn't understand it till I'm ready. Rather like trying to understand physics without the learning process. He emphasises knowing the rules – [§ he seems to be having trouble with the word, he doesn't know whether to say level or vibration] – knowing the rules of the level or vibration you're on. Find I have to keep maintaining my interest on this level.

*You mean the earth level?*

Yes. Very easy to slip away from it.

*This is because you've got a job to do here?*

Yes. My love and interest keep me in touch. If not for this it would be very easy to slip away. Find also using words clumsy. Didn't expect to feel this so much.

*Is it because you're wanting to use telepathy all the time?*

Thoughts convey more, more expression. Putting it into words now seems very clumsy. I am making progress but fear slowly.

*What is time?*

No sense of time but feel as if I'm doing everything in slow motion.

*I expect that's because half of you is really on a higher vibration.*

Possibly, or maybe I haven't adjusted enough.

§ In the old days there was a way of rating you as a medium, it never let you get sloppy. We should bring it back.

It would be an important crusade because we're in danger of becoming too frightened to push for a standard, and it's the ones at the top that are preventing it because they would be most indignant at being tested or supervised, and yet discipline is needed. I have gone round some circles, and watched some communications from this side. It's sloppily done. I'm amazed at how patient spirit is in accepting this but it has been pointed out to me that some gets through. People need to be taught not to put mediumship on a fortune-telling level. I have watched mediums being allowed, even been encouraged, by the sitter to talk about material things because others are doing it. Sitting should be about spirit's evidence of survival, some help for the sitter's soul to make progress, not about new house or job. I look back and wish I had stated these moves before I left. I tried!

47

*What did you come up against?*

I know they thought I was old-fashioned. I used to get complaints that I wasn't writing about this one or that one. I had started to delegate authority shortly before I passed and although I had the final word I wanted to encourage the others for when I wasn't there. But sometimes I feel I led them in the wrong direction; no, didn't lead – allowed them to go in the wrong direction. Conan understands, have discussed it with him. He understands, as a writer can understand, why interpretation is everything. Have discussed it with Silver Birch. He spoke of allowing people to find their own path. He said the spirit within us recognises truth, values integrity, understands the need for discipline. He says we have to give people the opportunity to exercise their spiritual knowledge. So maybe my campaign would not be a good thing. I am unsure of this. Nevertheless I fear this wandering off, away from the essential truths, and I do not want something I created for spirit either to encourage such wandering off or aid and abet it. I do know this, if it wanders off in a tangent it will still be with the best of motives. I look back at the way I was before I passed and I was already begining to wander off. We once argued about it, I didn't accept it. [§ He says can you remember?]

*Not precisely, unfortunately, but I don't doubt we did.*

§ You implied his paper had lost its bite. That it wasn't the serious though kind onlooker. He did resent it and felt you were wrong at the time but now he says, 'No. I was beginning to wander off to look for what was sensational rather than what would teach, what would give understanding.'

## EIGHT

## 9TH NOVEMBER 1984

The fog is clearing. I'm talking about myself. Thought with my previous knowledge it would be easier for me but discovered that preconceived ideas can create a fog. Wasn't flexible enough. Thought I was but was surprised to discover how I cling, or clung, to certain ways of thinking.

*Natural enough.*

Got to be careful with that over here because then you create your own reality and you're seeing what you want to see and doing what you want to do. You said to me once I was getting rigid in my ideas, can you remember?

*Well it was certainly my opinion.*

You said it. Didn't realise you were right, only realised it over here. Asked Silver Birch why he didn't put me right. He said you had to discover that for yourself. I'm amazed at some of the others over here, never heard of them, yet some are doing better than I am. Think they must have been old souls.

*Well it's like a family; once you catch up it doesn't make any difference does it?*

There can be backward members in the family.

49

*I'm not classing you with those.*

§ He just laughs.

Never mind, let us gird up our loins and go on to pastures new. I'm beginning to realise the difficulties spirit had with us and the frustration. Hard work. Am already experiencing some difficulty remembering certain things about my earth life. Didn't expect this to happen so quickly. Always prided myself on my memory.

*Yes, but then the spring has gone now hasn't it, the motive for it really?*

Yes but it makes it difficult communicating, when wanting to draw things back to memory to give as evidence.

*Yes I well see.*

See a lot of our old comrades.

*Do you work as a group or is it an individual matter?*

Individual matter. Got to know more about ourselves before we can do that. Amazing the silly things that haunt you over here. Keep reviewing an incident with one of my reporters that I handled wrongly. Finding I do this quite a bit sometimes, go over certain incidents, review them from different angles, try to be totally honest. Not accept excuses from myself.

*Yes indeed. Does he want to name the reporter or would he prefer not to?*

You know the one. We broke up and went our separate ways. You know who I mean.

*Yes I know who he means. A bit obstinate.*

Yet I handled it wrong, wrongly – [§ he keeps correcting me when I say wrong.]

50

*He means the one who threw away an opportunity, is that right?*

§ Yes. Grooming for stardom. He says that should tell you who he means.

*Yes it does.*

§ Looking back realise we could have worked something out.

*Pity.*

Know I'm not responsible for him but on the other hand with different handling we could both have achieved more.

*I expect I shall find some of those little lucky dips when it's my turn to come over.*

You will. It's like highlights, crossroads, periods when your life could have gone this way or that way. Depending on your realisation and awareness.

§ He says I didn't approve of him, that I thought he didn't do a good job of promoting integrity and dignity. But he says he did the best he could for Spiritualism. That was a personal comment.

I'm getting better at this.

*Yes, you are a bit more fluent, better footwork I would say.*

Seems I have to hold tight onto the medium.

*Well she's very worth holding on to.*

Not let it slip away. Amusing really. Never knew her except through paper. Think that's why better contact, no pretending to be me. Have tried to reach you through other mediums, not good.

51

*I realise the difficulty only too well and no doubt that's why he tried to conceal himself in the early days. Did one recently describe you as if it were a priest I knew in my young days?*

Yes.

*Ah I never thought that was you. But I can see the description applies quite well.*

You understand?

*Yes.*

I gave up because it was coming through all wrongly. You understand? I just backed off then. If you'll notice, it never went really any further.

*No that's right.*

Once it started to go wrong I backed off.

*Yes, I see. She's promising though, in my view.*

Yes but she's not listening.

*Yes – the old story eh?*
*He's already said that his old peers with whom he worked weren't yet working together as a group because, he implied, they weren't sufficiently at one or sufficiently advanced. Does he want to say any more about that? It's a frequent complaint that not enough of these former leaders come back in an effective way.*

I understand that. I haven't reached that state myself yet but I'm already noticing with my memories that there is a fading.

*This needs to be better known.*

The best I can liken it to is like some good friends going

to another country. At first there is constant contact and then they get interested in the other country.

I don't know if it's right or wrong that they do this. I don't think I will do it but I don't know.

*To let the interest fade you mean?*

Yes.

*You hope not to?*

I hope not to.

*But you see how easy it can be?*

I think I realise more now how dedicated guides have to be. Remember I have returned and spoken and not everybody's listening, it can be very discouraging.

*Yes.*

§ He's laughing and saying 'You become old news'. He corrects me at times when I'm speaking to you and I knows he's using these words because they're better for me, not for him. Much in the same way as I would use certain words for a child, you know, to keep it simple and short.

*Well this is the art of communicating through a sensitive isn't it?*

## NINE

## 12TH DECEMBER 1984

I continue to make progress. One finds one's point of view is changing, that all terms are relative. Find it very difficult now to remember anything to do with my passing. I really hate to think about it.

*Well it was all so quick anyway wasn't it?*

§ Yes but he talks about the dreamlike quality of this world.

*Of his world?*

§ No this world.

*Our world?*

§ He describes it as making yourself keep in touch, as if it would be too easy to lose that contact. He's speaking of making a conscious effort. He can understand why we never hear from some people when they come over here. They have not made that effort to remain in touch.

*Our mutual friend – and he'll know whom I mean – is surprised that Barbie hasn't by now gone off into a world of glory and light.*

§ He's laughing. He's discovered you make your own glory and light and if it's not in you it's not anywhere. He talks about it being in the eye of the beholder.

*Well our friend reckons that the life Barbie led on earth and the work he did would have entitled him to that, but I don't myself agree with that way of reckoning it.*

§ He's shaking his head and he says he's not being modest. Over here you really see what you achieved and, what is more important, the motives behind it, some of which he wasn't always aware of at the time. It's not a case of being humble, but the experience is humbling. There has been a period where he felt almost disgusted with himself for some of his motives.

*I've no doubt we all feel that at times when we get over there.*

§ But he says he was told that this is a sign of awareness. The more aware you are, the more aware your judgement of yourself. This is why some souls over here seem quite content, while others experience a certain amount of anguish.

*So the ones who are content are awaiting their turn?*

Yes. The greater your knowledge, the greater your judgement of yourself. You appreciate the finer points. However I'm not unhappy over here, I have come through that period of disgust and realised it is a refining process. Having always been someone in the past who gave the news, I am trying from this level to evaluate and hand on the understanding that I am gaining.

*Will you need quite a number of talks to put this across to me?*

I think so. In explaining it to you I am testing my own understanding of it. Our friend may be disappointed and think things are not as rosy as we had expected them to be, but I must confess I find this way more exciting.

*Be a bit boring otherwise wouldn't it?*

There is constantly the urge to understand more. [§ He changed the word, urge, to hunger.]

*Who are his main companions now? In the deeper sense?*

Our friend Myers but I don't see him often. Sometimes spend some time with Harry and Gordon. As you know I'm closer to one than the other. Ena is good company.

*She's found her feet pretty quickly by the sound of it?*

Yes but I feel their type of work has tended to leave them in some ways unlearned in their own soul's advancement.

*Well having to be the public figure doesn't lead to self-knowledge much does it?*

This is what I mean. And so there is this lack of awareness and understanding which you and I who have been more contemplative have gained.

*Swings and roundabouts.*

Yes. Remember, although you have had a guide on your level, coming to this world is rather like going out of school, leaving school. Although your teacher is still there for some help, you must start to accomplish by yourself. This is not to say that we never see them.

*Our mutual friend was surprised that you weren't practically at one with yours.*

No, I have much to achieve before that.

*What name do you call him by these days?*

Still the same name but I am beginning to become aware of other roles he has played.

56

*In your past or just in general?*

In general. At one time I thought of him as being a higher Self but no, I am quite distinct from him, but I did consider at one time, if this could be possible. But I find he speaks for a more highly developed group.

*Yes. And does he have the same name in that group too?*

No.

*Is he able to tell me the name in that group or would he prefer not to?*

§ Barbanell keeps taking me down the stairs and showing me the glass book-case. Are there books down there that refer to Stainton Moses?

*Does he mean that the same guide was behind both Stainton Moses and himself, or a different aspect?*

§ No, similar.

*Would he say someone of the same basic spiritual group then?*

§ Yes.

*So there's a common task and maybe others will come along, all have a go in turn. Is he suggesting this?*

§ Yes. It's difficult for him to explain because he is still trying to understand it completely himself.

*I see.*

§ But he does speak of not just the one, you understand?

*Yes.*

§ One voice but not just the one.

57

*It's very mysterious isn't it?*

§ No, it's just that he hasn't got all the answers yet. He's groping towards them.

*It makes one wonder where one leaves off.*

§ He speaks of blurring. As if it's not as clearly defined as we would want it to be.

*Ask him how Silver Birch chose that name.*

§ He talks about Silver Birch as a pseudonym. He's talking about wisdom and age and philosophy. I don't know what he's getting at. But he says he only got half the answer when he was on earth and not the whole answer. He says I'm blocking him but I'm not. It's to do with Silver Birch's identity.

*Yes, that's right. But as you say it's still an incomplete answer.*

§ Yes but he's blaming me for that.

*Oh that's a bit tough isn't it?*

§ He says I'm not picking him up right. This is where he finds it very frustrating. He is limited by the instrument, meaning me.

*By the sitter too of course.*

§ He tries to put it on a clever level so it cannot be put down to telepathy.

## TEN

## DATE UNKNOWN

I find sometimes my thought processes rambling over such a wide spectrum of possible realities that I find I have to exercise discipline and control over them.

*So that you don't put too much on your plate at once as it were?*

Exactly. As if too much on my plate, as you would say, would be too much to focus upon and thereby it would become blurred. Truly the possibilities of this level are all embracing and one can only expand one's consciousness a little bit at a time. To gulp them too much would be to lead to indigestion. There is at times a feeling of disorientation, not as much as in the past but still a little bit. It gives you the feeling that things at times are not quite as solid as they seem. It does not cause distress or unhappiness. I would rather describe it as things not quite seen, just out of range of your eyes, flickerings, flickerings at the side of your eyes, yet when looked at are not there. This is the kind of disorientation I speak of.

## ELEVEN

## 15TH JANUARY 1985

§ He's settling in better. He talks about an awareness increasing.

*Is it like opening up the aura?*

§ Yes, being more aware for longer periods. Looking back at first he was only aware for short periods, then there appeared to be periods where he would be in a sort of dream state.

*He mentioned those.*

§ Although he is dragged back with thoughts of this world, and lots of people he cares about, he is finding it increasingly difficult to see as important certain things taking place on earth that would normally have been of the utmost importance to him.

*I see. Is he talking about organisational things?*

Yes. There is still an interest there but not to the same degree. There is not the emotional involvement that once there was. I am losing my sense of time and so there are times when I am only aware of your visit by your thoughts. [§ He is asking if you understand this?]

*Yes, I think I do, it's like ringing him up on the 'phone telepathically.*

§ He's nodding.

*Well he still arrives at the right time and the right place.*

Yes but I'm beginning to feel as if I'm split in two, as if part of me is in your time and part of me is in the time that I now exist in.

*Does that mean that when you are in my time only a part of you can speak?*

No, as far as I know all of me speaks.

*All of you, good.*

And yet it's as if I'm not completely here.

*Very strange, isn't it?*

It feels comfortable enough but difficult to describe. It's as if I have a foot in both worlds, in both time phases and I am straddling the two. I cannot say I am not here with you but I'm also there. I was not so much aware of this previously.

§ He says to me, 'I know, my dear, you have not been very happy at the beginning of this link-up with me, feeling that there is not a lot we have in common. Nevertheless you have been prepared to let me speak. And I do feel your reluctance rather than your enthusiasm has been good for the experiment. For someone who would have been enthusiastic would not have served my purpose.'

*Your purpose being?*

To identify myself and not have words put in my mouth.

*So the reluctance could have been of value in that?*

It was of value. Reluctance was not resistance and so

61

there was no effort to please me or to set herself up as an oracle of mine. Slowly this reluctance has given way but there is still a hesitancy there that we still have very little in common. This serves my purpose still for had I spoken through someone who agreed totally and was on the same level, it would then have been hard to distinguish what was mine and what was theirs.

*Yes I quite see the point you're making. You'd have come out more like the old Barbie wouldn't you?*

Yes but how much would there have been of the real me? I have even had to alter to a certain degree my way of speaking, and have used phrases and terms that would be acceptable to the medium. Much in the same way as one adjusts one's conversation to various people. This has caused some of my old friends to be unsure that it is myself who is speaking, but surely the type of thinking behind the words is still recognisable?

*I would have thought so.*

Just as this medium did not resist or reject me so I felt I had to play my part in the partnership I hope to develop. As you can understand there has to be give and take on both sides.

*What part does her guide, the little Japanese lady, play in this?*

Once she realised that I was competent and knew what I was doing and was aware enough not to distress, then she very kindly stepped back, and allowed me free access but of course some of my success in this direction was because she knew of my work with that higher soul. I do not know if I would have found it so easy. However because she knew of the work that I and another had done this enabled her to trust me.

*I'm interested in all this question of how communicators are located.*

There are several ways. One of course is your telepathic telephone call which prepares me, for as you know we don't know time in your terms. Another way is the emotional tug where there has been tremendous unhappiness.

*Through the passing you mean?*

Yes or around the person left on earth which emotionally will pull those closest to them. Third way of course is an intellectual exercise.

*That seems very difficult to me.*

For which you need the co-operation and agreement of spirit to take part. There is a tendency among some, not yourself included, to play tricks with us which is deeply resented but where intelligence, integrity and the open outlook of the scientist is concerned, with the agreement of spirit it can be done. As you can understand we do not like performing party tricks. It is of no credit to us nor to the sitter. So the third means of communication must be done with the co-operation of spirit, with the right attitude and with reasoned judgement. Where this is concerned what you are looking for can be achieved, but like any experiment it must be set up carefully and with all parties knowing what is going on. When that has taken place, and a time, a mode of communication and a link created, then it is no longer looking for a needle in a haystack, it is like a beam reaching out only to one possible person. [§ He shows me a beam of light.]

Sometimes it is like saying to someone who comes to Britain: Look up so and so when you're in England, with only a name and a place. I know those on the higher levels

63

can be very clever and do such things but I am a newcomer, I'm a beginner, I'm a learner. I find since I have come to this level that even the most sincere enquirer does not talk enough to us directly. I am putting this badly. They expect us to read their thoughts and anticipate what they want but they do not give us the courtesy of informing us. They say to themselves you're in spirit, you should know I am doing this, even though they themselves do not contact and expressly ask this. This is the reason sometimes communication is rejected, through a presumption which they would not make on this level that you're on. A presumption that it is enough that *they* want it.

*Too true. The medium thought you had more to say about the subject of our last talk about the Old Man. Is that going to come in the future or have you really finished?*

No I will speak more as I learn more.

*Right. I felt a strange inward satisfaction when you were speaking of him, as if something in me endorsed it.*

I felt the same. His hallmark was there but what an unusual role.

*Yes indeed.*

I feel I have only been given a glimpse of a facet of him but yes, I will speak more when I know more.

*To medium: 'I wonder if you find it as interesting as I do?'*

§ Sometimes when I know what he's talking about but other times he does lose me because it's something between you and him and I don't know what I'm talking about.

64

*And sometimes I think he is purposely covering it up.*

§ Yes I think he does because he feels then I've really got to go by his words rather than put my own words in. He likes it best when I'm letting him actually say the words to me, rather than saying: he says such and such. He seems to worry that I'll start putting bits on.

*Yes, of course this is where the mind begins to pop up doesn't it?*

§ And so he doesn't like it when I do it that way. Whenever he gets the chance I feel he is saying, 'Just sit there and repeat what I tell you to say.'

## TWELVE

## 8TH FEBRUARY 1985

§ Maurice Barbanell shakes his head and says, 'Oh dear you've put your foot in it again.' According to him it's something you've said recently.

*I can guess the person I was talking to.*

§ And he's laughing.

I appreciate what you were trying to do but I doubt if he did. It's a terrible thing when you have to start guarding your tongue. I found this towards the end. People thought I was becoming complacent but I wasn't. I just didn't see the point, it wouldn't have done any good. I am constantly meeting people over here who say they expected me to be on a higher level. Words to this effect: 'I didn't expect to see you here.' This is getting rather boring! I inform them that I only worked for spirit, that at times my own progress was neglected.

*It seems a bit of a contradiction.*

One constantly realises over here that more time should have been spent in contemplation. I can understand now why in the past those who achieved spiritual advancement on the earth level, had to go off by themselves, for in helping others there is sacrifice, but I do not regret anything.

*Your friend still finds it hard to accept that you didn't go straight up to the top floor; I think he considers it as a rebuff to him somewhere, although he doesn't say so.*

Our understanding on this level here is limited although we may think it isn't. Our spiritual side works on this level on earth. Should be done with no hope of reward.

*Absolutely.*

If done in the other way we achieve nothing. I look back and realise there were times when I was consciously spiritual rather than being spiritual. There is a difference.

*Yes there is.*

I am beginning to learn the real meaning of the word humble, because as I look back there are periods I handled wrongly. To be truly spiritual one does not do it in a conscious fashion. There is no decision, for there can only be one way. Over here you learn to examine your actions very carefully. There were times when I was not patient, when I was not kind in its truest and best meaning. My guide and mentor said to me recently: 'Have you learned to serve yet?' Serve those who are not as aware and understanding as oneself. As you know I did not have a lot of patience with slow-thinking people. When this was said I realised what was meant. I find it difficult to explain my feelings, yet what was being said was that one greater than I was able to do this for me. [§ He asks if you understand?]

*Yes I think so. In reducing himself so as to be Barbie's instrument. Is that what he means?*

Yes. Can you see me reducing myself, my friend?

*It's a bit hard, Barbie.*

67

Yet I have the feeling it is the only path. What is it that was said, you must lose yourself to gain yourself. I haven't lost myself, not enough.

§ He's finding it difficult to speak of this, Paul. I don't know if it is because of what words to use to explain it or whether it is emotionally.

*Yes. I'm wholly by his side.*

§ I can't make up my mind which is bothering him most.

Still I think I have advanced enough to see the mistakes.

*Do you feel all the time round you a light or an influence or a feeling that kindles you so to speak, kindles your spiritual self?*

Yes but it also exposes. I can best describe it as a mirror and a dim light and then a mirror and a bright light. In the dim light you do not see the imperfections although they are there. In this bright loving understanding light you look in the mirror and feel ashamed, yet no one says anything, nor is there any judgement or criticism. Somehow that makes it worse.

*I hope you don't forget the credits all the same.*

There is this tremendous hunger, urge to achieve, urge to attain. Can you remember periods where for a brief moment everything seemed clear?

*Yes, they're very few and far between though.*

But can you remember the feeling of those moments?

*Yes I can.*

Well imagine them for a longer period but not

permanent, and you have an idea of the hunger and the urge.

*Yes I see.*

But let us not speak so dolefully, my friend.

*It's not really doleful is it?*

These are my personal problems. I am becoming very self-conscious – [§ but that wasn't the word he used] – I am becoming very conscious of my self indulgence and so try to prevent it. Tell our mutual friend, he is looking to his own future and wondering. Tell him this is why I am a disappointment to him. How could I become part of a Gestalt until I learn to serve? I was corrected the other day when I spoke of a higher level. I was told this was an earth expression.

*What should you have said then? An inner level?*

§ He's trying to give me the word he . . .

I was told there was no higher or lower levels, only greater depth and awareness. They said that to speak of a higher level encouraged arrogance. They spoke of a shift of perception. They were not angry with me over this, it was pointed out as a childish concept which made me feel embarrassed. I had made the mistake of asking and speaking of the higher levels. How one could be aware of them, how could one achieve them? It was pointed out to me first that my expression was wrong, my imagery, that there was no up or down but *there*, that as my perception changed and shifted so the scene would change. It was pointed out to me that only my own thoughts held me back, that my conceptions and awareness were the blocks. Can you understand?

*Yes, I can feel your hunger too.*

69

It is very difficult, not unpleasant, but difficult.

*I suppose these difficulties dissolve at a particular moment and you're suddenly there?*

Yes. I am used to working to a plan, a formula, but it doesn't work that way.

*No. Good old Taurus eh?*

I am used to thinking in terms of: you do this, you achieve that – it doesn't work that way. I can understand why; though they say it is basically simple, we make it complicated.

*It takes a genius or a fool to be simple doesn't it?*

As was said to me in my hunger, 'As you think, you *are*.' Which I know, yet making it work is difficult. I am not shocked at what I have learned, but surprised and with the feeling that I could kick myself.

*And no doubt you're the person who is hardest on yourself.*

Probably. I have always been in a hurry. And now that I have glimpsed what is possible I am in even more of a hurry.

*Whatever does Swaff think of you?*

He is amused.

*Hope he's not 'telling' you quite so much.*

He says that always I want to outreach everybody else. He did speak of his concern over conditions on earth, the young souls, the burden that has been placed upon them. He said each generation has its problems but the generation that is coming now has bigger problems than have been in the past but then that is typical of him. We still have our friendly arguments which neither wins. It is enjoyable.

*Thank you very much for the talk which I deeply appreciate.*

§ He says that wasn't a talk, that was an unburdening of the soul in the true meaning of the word.

## THIRTEEN

## 5TH JUNE 1985

§ Barbanell's standing here. Your lady* won't come. She's very busy at the moment trying to work things out for herself.

*Oh well good.*

She's trying to deal with it intellectually and it won't work.

*Same old problem.*

She's trying to apply the old rules to the new situation. [§ He also adds that she's very rigid in her thinking and this isn't helping matters.] She didn't have a lot of time for religion on this level.

*No she didn't.*

Although that is not necessarily a drawback, in her case it has become one for some reason.

*I can understand that.*

§ He feels sorry for her, she's very mixed up and confused.

*I don't think she'd much like one feeling sorry for her either.*

* When on earth, a member of the Society for Psychical Research.

§ He's laughing. He says, 'Oh, I haven't told her. You'll only hear from her when she's got this sorted out.' As if she has to deal with this first.

*Yes, very understandable.*

§ He's not sure if she believes in communication, even though, he says, it's been proven to her that it can be done because she's done it.

*Since she died he means?*

Yes. She did it before but she didn't really approve of doing it. She did it with a certain reluctance, which you must have been conscious of at the time.

*No surprise.*

Rather like doing something that you consider rather lowbrow.

*Yes. But if you can't be a medium yourself you can't call it lowbrow really can you?*

This lady can.

I myself continue to make slow progress, I'm not even sure if I should call it that. It is hard to judge. I still find myself evaluating a lot of what I've done, and my own thoughts. This level makes you very introspective.

*Is that why many people seem to do this process in private and we don't hear from them while they're doing it?*

Yes. Nevertheless there is always the understanding between us that we would continue to report progress whichever one of us went first.

*And it's valuable.*

I can understand now very clearly why some do not return. It is such a private matter, this sorting oneself out.

73

Also it is so difficult to explain the process. Already I am beginning to find words clumsy. This medium suits me because I have to put words in simple form.

*Well she's been very faithful, hasn't she, for you?*

She accepts the way I want to speak. I stopped her with the 'he says' and 'she says' at the beginning.

*That's right.*

She still does this.

*Well it's difficult enough being a medium without facing a blue pencil as well isn't it?*

True but I have told her it is a bad habit so maybe my blue pencil is helping her.

*They transcribe well on the whole.*

That is why I have made her do it this way, I knew what was needed.

I have briefly seen Myers, with the Old Man but he's here there and everywhere.

*Myers is?*

Yes, rushing around. I have to use these terms although they are physical terms.

*He wants to keep a finger on everything I suppose?*

Yes, still.

*Well he's still a bit of a hero to me you know.*

Always was, more than to me. I felt he scattered too far and wide, too bitty at times.

*I would have thought it was part of his integrity not to let anything pass by.*

Yes, I can see that now. All things were considered, all possibilities, but I feel at one period he should concentrate more on one field rather than several. Have seen C.D.

*Have you?*

Has been rather unhappy.

*Why is that?*

Says they speak of him as having been naïve, forget the good bits; frightened the gold will be buried in the dross, you understand?

*Yes. Why he is still worried about that, it's all such a long while ago?*

Because he feels he did more harm than good now.

*I see.*

He said it looks as if he misdirected people rather than directed them.

*Well he made some very good statements via Grace Cooke, didn't he, to put that right?*

Yes, but they don't remember these.

*Really? It sounds as if he's a bit fixated on this bit of his past then?*

He's yet to forgive himself for his bumbling, bungling. He does not allow the unhappiness over this to weigh too much with him, rather something that niggles him. A reminder. I've told him we all make these mistakes.

*If it's not one it's another isn't it?*

I have a few I look back on with regret. Things I should have done to keep things going in straight lines.

75

*Presenting too simple a picture really.*

C.D. was always sensitive.

*Sensitive, yes.*

To criticism.
Find difficulty regarding time matching it with yours.
This is a new difficulty.

*A new difficulty for you, you mean?*

Yes.

*Because you can't forecast with any confidence?*

Not yet. Later will be able to do this.

*Is this a special skill to be acquired then?*

Different concept. Time flowing like a stream. Difficult getting in on the right period of it. Don't know if this medium knows it but I have been improving her understanding of spirit.

*How have you done that?*

Thought when she saw babies in spirit that they were babies, did not realise she was being shown a picture. Made her realise that such a spirit must return. Not always at once, but eventually. Making it difficult for her now to speak of babies growing up in spirit world, have stopped her doing this. Made her realise that she must try and explain this to the sitter.

*Very difficult.*

Made her realise that no baby is a personal property that can only belong to those parents. She is finding trouble explaining this in a modified manner to people she works with. I did not do this to cause upset but felt as the

76

contact between us had linked up more strongly, could start to teach her a little bit. Don't know if she likes this. Of course there is advantage in this to me also. As she becomes more knowledgeable I can work better. So have not done this with altruistic motive: we both benefit. Gave you this one example to show you areas I have been improving knowledge in, missing links I'm linking up.

*Are you and a lot of the pioneers getting together to present a better image than this image that's been presented for so long?*

Yes. Several of us are involved in this.

*Good.*

We feel we should mend bridges before we move on, so that others will be able to walk over but there will be a lot of opposition.

*Oh without doubt.*

You are already meeting it now. Expect scurrilous attacks, but we've coped with those before.

## FOURTEEN

## 12TH JULY 1985

I can understand why people at a certain level over here start to draw back.

It hasn't happened to me yet but I can understand why they see us like children playing games, as if they're the adults and they let us get on with playing games. Can understand why people pull back from this level and find that there is not a lot we can explain. I, because I am stubborn and persevere, will continue but others feel that the gap becomes too wide. My own perception of the level I am on comes and goes. I'm wondering if I am in for a change, a shift. It is like a shift of light but it's not, it's more than that, it's a shift of emphasis. Could you understand this?

*Yes perfectly well.*

It is not uncomfortable, only distressing. I have seen our friend.

*The Old Fellow?*

He grows in stature. I'm almost afraid to approach him now. It was easier when I was in your world, now I am seeing the reality. He lectures us at times and yet lecture isn't the right word.

*He shares his mind?*

Yes but I can only understand one in ten things, the rest I grasp at feebly. It can be very frustrating. I do feel more strongly this shift in my perspective, and wonder what lies ahead, and if I can handle it.

*Well I don't think it would come to you unless you could handle it.*

That is what I've been told. I would never have described myself as having rigid views but in comparison to what I've been shown it makes my views seem rigid.

It has been a salutary lesson.

*I suspected this morning the Old Fellow had got a lot of his original wisdom from China?*

He told us wisdom *is*. All have the opportunity to reach for it. Reality *is*. Wisdom is reality. Each person, each religion reaches towards the same truth. When that truth is reached it belongs to no one or is started by no one, it merely *is*. All take different paths to it. If I give you a truth which you then hold to and, in another country, another time, someone recognises the truth that you have spoken of, his recognition of your truth makes he and you on the same level. It doesn't matter which direction it came from, or even if it was known by another because it doesn't change. The reason I say this is because already this was spoken of to the Old Man. This question was raised and his answer was this: 'I can share my mind with you but if your mind is not on my level or I have not portrayed that truth in its right context then it will mean nothing to you. I might as well have shown you nothing.' He neither accepted nor rejected the issue of where his wisdom came from. I could say he was indifferent to it. He merely said to the one who brought this up: 'Do not clutter your mind with trivia.' So I thought I would mention this to you.

79

*Yes, thank you.*

There are people of thought that we gather around. This is the best way I can describe this to you. There is one pool of thought where the teacher or master just keeps repeating one question. I have not myself taken much interest in this.

*Why not?*

Because I am drawn to the Old Fellow, but I have heard that the question which is repeated again and again is: 'Who are you?' Nothing more and, according to what I have heard, as your awareness increases your answer changes. I have not asked the Old Man what he thinks of this. I do not think he would comment anyway. I have also been aware of Myers but only for a brief occasion.

*Do you know why you saw him just then?*

Yes. I was thinking of him and wondering what he was up to. Never a man to be still. When we met it was rather dreamlike. It seemed real in so many ways, yet unreal in others. He spoke of scientists in his world getting together to help your world. He seemed very excited but I felt it wouldn't work.

*I think it needs scientists on our side who care enough.*

Myers seemed to think that his scientists could stimulate yours.

*I see.*

But I didn't feel it would work. Being on the level we are I could not hide this thought from him, but it did not seem to disturb him. He is a man who often gets very excited and when he's off on a scheme, a plan, he doesn't listen to others.

80

I thought you would want to know he has not changed.

*Yes. I'm interested.*

I had caught your thought and spoken to him of the Gestalt. He said he did not believe a group of souls could be as effective as he felt he could be as an individual. He must remain as he is to achieve this.

*The experiment's still worth doing though.*

Myers is too much of an individualist for this. This is something I know and you know he would be most reluctant to give up. I could not see him tying himself to the plodding minds of others; they wouldn't be plodding but they would seem like that to him.

*I would take it that the White Eagle we know, is an aspect of a greater soul just as Silver Birch was the aspect of a greater soul?*

Yes.

*What sort of spiritual link is there between these great beings? Just by virtue of what they are I suppose?*

The link between these great beings lay in the fact that they both wished to help and guide at this level but both were different entities. Just as the Old Gentleman portrayed himself in a different racial garb, so the same was true of White Eagle.

I do know that the entity that was White Eagle, and is still White Eagle, had an existence in your world that came from the East. If certain of his words are looked at, the Eastern outlook is there.

*Are you in touch with Grace Cooke?*

Grace is becoming increasingly difficult to be in touch with.

81

*Because she's going on you mean?*

She seems to become distant, as if she's relating to you on one level but linking on another, almost as if she too is developing an aspect.

*Yes, I see.*

It is like speaking to someone who speaks with one part of themselves but the other part is a long way away. This is becoming more obvious.

*What of your old friend?*

He expected miracles from me when I came over! He feels I've let him down. This is not so. If he has to rely on me for his faith and trust then it has not been good enough. Would you agree? He expected much from me.

*Yes, he did and quite apart from expecting much in the spiritual sense he wanted very exact proof that I think really it's not possible to get.*

It could be done.

*It could be done?*

I could do it.

*But you don't think it's wise to do it?*

I think I would be helping him cheat at an exam.

*I see, yes.*

I look and realise that if I gave him so much, he would want more and this could be a never-ending thing.

## FIFTEEN

## 22ND MARCH 1985

*I am not satisfied with my book. I wanted to try and be more simple but this has proved difficult. I felt I was writing myself into something more complex and this I wanted to avoid.*

§ He's nodding his head and he says it's the same over here, the simplest things seem the difficult things.

I have sometimes wished that I was on the level of an Aunt Maggie type of spirit. They seem content with their lot. I have been blessed or cursed with an active mind that complicates things.

*I see I shall have a lot of chasing to do by the time I get over there.*

§ He's smiling, he says you have been warned.

It is a bit like your world where you see certain people gliding along not thinking very deeply about things and others tortured with self-doubt, self-analysis etc. I am of course as usual my cynical self. I try to judge my progress and find it difficult. Time, as I expected, is becoming difficult to judge. I was concerned about Sylvia but I'm happier now with things around her.

*Pity she can't come over to you.*

She wants to very much but she must be patient. She's trying to write a book you know.

*Is she? I wouldn't have thought it possible.*

It was something we discussed when I was on earth but she's left it too late. I and her mother and father are doing everything we can to make things easier for her. It is difficult, when you are in your world, to realise the struggle the spirit has sometimes to leave the body and this has been her problem. Still she's in good hands.

*Good.*

And we're always there if she needs us. Soon she will join us but not yet because she is becoming weaker, yet holding on to the body.

I have seen him briefly twice. His way of thinking is not mine. One could say we are not on each other's wavelength.

*Who is he talking about now that he's seen twice?*

§ He says there can only be one 'him' for him.

*Does he mean the wise Old Man?*

Yes.

*Oh I see and I'm all ears.*

I must say he is not as much help over here as he was in your world.

*Really? He's making you learn the hard way I gather?*

Yes. I spoke of him because I knew you would want to hear. I would not say our friend is unfriendly. His support to a degree is still there.

*What's the difficulty then?*

That I must reach up more to him now. He said he was making it easy for me on earth. I suppose one tends to think of him as personal property which of course he is not.

*No indeed.*

To think of him as one's teacher, who is special for you.

*When you throw that away you'll be nearer to him I imagine.*

Being in his presence makes one feel uncomfortable.

*That's interesting. Like being in the presence of the King with the wrong clothes on?*

Very much so. He tries to make it easy, but that sometimes seems more difficult for me then, as if he is having to adjust for me. Having done it myself to others in the past I recognise it.

When I am with him, although his attention is on me, the best way I can describe my feeling is as if he's looking at other horizons. [§ I don't feel I've explained that well. Neither does he, mind you, he doesn't feel he's expressed it properly.]

I feel very much a child in his presence and that he gives me a parent's humour. [§ He's happy with explaining it that way.]

*A parent's got other topics on his mind.*

Other things that the child cannot comprehend. And yet our friend essentially remains a simple man.

*This I could well believe.*

It is extraordinary that he had this effect even though he is a simple man. He did speak of his concern for the world that you live in, at this moment when there is a great deal of unhappiness and unrest. He said he and others were trying to help with this, to reach the right minds. Our friend would say that there is always pain in giving birth to new thoughts and new ideas, new ways of thinking.

*I take it we've both lost interest in S.J.R.C.*

Yes. He says his went before yours did. But I knew you would come round to my way of thinking.

*Well I think we both felt this a long time beforehand, we just persevered in a rather hopeless way.*

Looking back it served a purpose for a period; although a lot was not achieved, there were some interesting moments. Of course I knew the writing was on the wall when others took over, and it became theirs rather than a communal project. At that point I realised.

*There were not enough who cared really.*

I wouldn't say that; did not care in the way we did, yes I would agree with you, but they cared about putting it along their lines, that kind of caring. They were more interested in pushing it their way, formalising it where we were trying to stay free of that. Do you understand?

Though some of my communications may seem rather gloomy tell my dear friend not to let it worry him. I was never one to enjoy myself wholeheartedly. I always wanted to look on the other side.

*That didn't always appear so much.*

It was there, you caught glimpses of it, both of you did. Tell him in many ways I am enjoying myself, but this urge to strive, to know as much as possible, is tremendous and he knows me well enough to know that I would rise to the challenge and want to know more and expect to do better.

86

It is difficult for me to explain this urge to know more, this hunger which makes me at times seem gloomy. As I said earlier, it would have been easier to be an Auntie Maggie type of spirit, one who accepted and enjoyed this much better life and existence over here, but always I must strive further.

*Then you were a worthy pupil of the Old Boy.*

I wish I could be content just to visit relatives, to speak to old friends, to potter away, but it is not me and, as you say, would he have chosen me if I had been like this?

*I don't think so.*

I never have been content with doing things the easy way. I think these meetings with the Old Man makes me realise how much more there is to be attained and instead of being defeated by it and rather gloomy at times about it, which I am, it makes me strive more, wanting to achieve it.

## SIXTEEN

## 11TH SEPTEMBER 1985

Am finding that my ideas are constantly changing.

*That's always good news to me.*

A bit difficult.

*A bit like wearing two suits of clothes at the same time?*

No, more like the ground under your feet not being solid. I notice that when my ideas go through a change, surroundings seem to alter. The Old Man isn't much help to me at this point.

*He leaves you alone for a good reason no doubt?*

Yes. Have to work these things out for myself.

*Don't you get help from anybody?*

Sometimes. Feel as if I'm fitting bits of a jigsaw puzzle together. Help comes from others who have been more advanced in their thinking. Find this difficult to explain.

*I don't feel your experience is altogether typical. Would you say it was?*

I don't know. It is relative to me. I know everything is relative to me. Maybe their descriptions differ. I know there was talk of people going to places of learning. Haven't been aware of that myself. Don't know if that means that I am advanced or I'm not ready for that.

*I would think it's just not the right time for it, that you've got important matters on hand to finish first. After all you're representative of a great deal in this movement aren't you? So maybe you have to be on the stage for many other people.*

Don't feel very proud of that at the moment. Experiencing a feeling of shame.

*Why shame?*

Looking at certain things I promoted or allowed to happen and didn't speak out strongly enough. When I look at confusion that now exists not much to be a representative of.

*Point taken.*

Now understand feeling of shame. Look at the movement I was part of here and feel it scattering, with pockets here and there of genuine good truth. Don't mean to sound dismal, merely trying to explain, ideas changing, scales falling from eyes. Have met some of our friends over here recently.

*It seems as if you're getting together for some sort of plan?*

I do know we are struggling towards some sort of self-knowledge and reality. Help each other now and again; discuss. Sometimes don't feel too bad when I realise they are on same path, same level but sometimes feel annoyed with myself that I haven't made more progress.

*Well it's a sign of sensitivity isn't it? That you feel that way?*

Yes. Find your world sometimes more difficult to reach, denser, hurtful.

89

*Well that surely implies progress on your part?*

Or a guilty conscience! Certain unformulated feelings and ideas regarding the spirit world I have not shared because I couldn't put them into words.

*No, you have to let them shape themselves for a while haven't you, inside you?*

Almost as if taking a leap forward blindly. And I am treading cautiously.

*I quite understand that.*

Myers' blind leap was not understood by others. We all tried to fit in and understand it but the concept, and the awareness needed, was lacking. It is almost as if we are approaching things from different angles. I don't feel being the representative of what many of us tried to do on this level an advantage. It seems to carry its own burden.

*Well everything with a pioneer edge to it carries a burden doesn't it?*

Yes but I look back, not often, but sometimes, and feel if I had done a better job there would not be this muddle and confusion that now exists and that you yourself are aware of. Why have you drawn back, my friend? For that very reason?

*I don't really know. I suppose I feel I can't say anything effective in the present climate.*

Yes but I was the one who set the climate up. I should have been more careful.

*But you didn't set it up as it has turned out to be.*

I will not let you justify me, old friend.

*It's a natural sentiment on my part.*

90

And kindly thought but not good for me.

*Right.*

I will not wallow in it, but accept it as the truth.

*And I'll kick you downstairs instead of upstairs, is that the idea?*

Not as much as I've kicked myself. Oh, I comfort myself by looking at the pockets of truth but I cannot claim a great deal of credit for those, they have largely happened by themselves. I think the thing that hurts me most is that those who are serious and dedicated to this truth no longer read what is written. I notice on this level that there are periods when I feel I am on the brink of some revelation but there are other periods where I feel very lethargic.

*Strange. I can understand the contrast but I wouldn't have thought you'd have felt lethargic, unless it's world vibrations that you're picking up. I don't think you meant that?*

No, not that type of lethargy. The type of lethargy that says: can I really reach up that far?

*I see.*

I know these are my own doubts but I cling to my periods of clarity where it seems a simple step. I did not realise that there could be doubts over here, but having spoken to the others realise that this is the remnant of the person we were there, the final sloughing off of the coat and so I do not feel so bad about it. One could describe it as periods of marvellous optimism and glimpses of what can be achieved and periods of pessimism. I have hopes that a group of us will have future work to do. In my optimistic moments I can almost catch sight of this.

*You mean work that will be translated on to the earth?*

Yes. As if each of us together can become a whole that is greater than any of us.

*Sure. This is one of the coming things isn't it?*

Possibly my periods of pessimism are because of the heights my optimism takes me. Basically our group is all more or less on the same level. Some seem a little bit more, some a little bit less, but we still have that mutual understanding and help that we offer each other. Sometimes I wonder if we are meant to do this.

*Oh surely.*

Help each other on. I think it could be possible.

*Those different angles which people in the group have will enrich the others?*

Yes and there have been periods when this has been helpful. All of them speak of regrets as they look back, and so my regrets become commonplace. It's almost as if we have to help each other out of this stage. It is the best way I can describe it. And I find my family links are more remote than the ones I have with the group. Although there are still links there. It is as if I am moving beyond family ties, which sometimes is hard to adjust to. Although I have spent some time with my relatives I find I have not got much in common with them and with some we are like polite strangers. Others in our group have noticed this also with their links. And so it must be a common situation.

*It's like a re-grouping towards one's true spiritual family?*

I think so. As was pointed out to me by one of our

group the body was given to you by those physical links, but that is no longer a link between you, and as that link has now dissolved so the family link of spirit comes into being, which is a separate thing entirely. There is some sentimental sadness attached to this but I have realised it for what it is and accept it.

## SEVENTEEN

## 12TH APRIL 1985

I find my lack of interest in certain things left behind is increasing. It is beginning to seem rather distant and far away. Not on every subject; where there is tremendous emotion that I have felt in the past, that interest remains.

*Do you think that'll go on or do you think that will fade into the background too?*

I think it will eventually fade, how long I don't know. One tends to be rather selfish over here, much more so.

*That's a surprise.*

At first I thought I was doing it wrongly but then it was explained to me that there were certain areas of myself that I must learn more about and explore more thoroughly. The prejudices and secret fears we have hidden, even from ourself, are amazing. In this degree one has to be selfish to turn within. Sometimes I look at the people on this level I am now on and feel a little bit frightened.

*Frightened?*

Our awareness is like a flickering candle, the flame must be carefully nurtured, it seems too easy to put out. Can you understand me, my friend?

94

*Pretty well I think, but purgation isn't really selfish at bottom is it?*

Well I always called a spade a spade. I find myself increasingly absorbed into making this flickering candle stronger. So much of what we are is not original but comes from our environment, our education, our fears and conditioned reflexes of thought. Amongst all this is your flickering candle. Awareness is the most precious thing you can have, totally in touch with reality and moving with it. This is why I spoke of fear. One imagines how easy it would be to be snuffed out, rather like clay on the potter's wheel, having not been strong enough to retain the shape. I am not telling you anything new, some of this you already know.

*It's very interesting to hear from someone in the middle of the experience.*

It is frightening, frightening in the sense of the soul being swamped, or our essence not being strong enough to remain, without being shattered by the experience. It is a challenge and the irony is the more one knows of this the more one fears, whereas others know no fear for they are not aware of the need. Truly ignorance is bliss. To the ones who communicate with their children, husbands, parents, whatever, there is no fear, they are quite happy and content to do this, but they do not look to the future of their own progress and one wonders if their reality is only tied up with those they've left behind, but they do not seem to grasp this. They seem to be content just to do this. Truly one must become very strong in the 'I' before you can give it up, the 'I' being you, the true person, not just the 'I' you are, in relationship to other people.

*Understood.*

95

Some people cannot exist without this identity that they receive from other people.

*In other words they cling.*

Yes. Observing them has been a very important lesson to me because I can see how easily one could fall into this trap. It's comfortable, it's comforting to others but it does nothing for you. Back to being selfish, but you understand.

*Oh yes.*

I mentioned to someone recently that I'm not very good at being humble and the answer was: 'We're not good enough yet to be humble.'

*Very good answer wasn't it?*

You know who would say that to me?

*Oh the Old Man I suppose.*

Yes.

*He's very subtle isn't he?*

We knew him when he wasn't so subtle, but he spoke that way then because of us and so I nurture my flame, dear friend. Maybe it is egotistical, this idea of being snuffed out, I do not know, I know only that I try.

*Well you've been around a long time so if you've escaped being snuffed out all this time you can't be too bad.*

§ He's quoting someone.

'The worst thing that can happen to you is to get what you want.'

*Myers.*

Having no physical discomforts or concerns, it is the mental level that causes the problems.

*Yes.*

There are very few of my old colleagues that I could speak to in this fashion.

*You mean those already on your side?*

No, on earth. If you think about this you will realise how right I am. I do not seek to malign them but they do not like to think uncomfortable thoughts. In this they have not grown as much as they should. They have that additional knowledge that others do not have, but with that additional knowledge they have still fallen into the trap of thinking of the spirit world as essentially a paradise, a place where one is rewarded. If you were to say this to them they would deny it but it is there, inherent in them.

*I well realise it.*

You have noticed this when you have spoken to them, and when they have rejected my discomfort. They would rather say it is not I who is speaking. Actually I have looked back and felt rather pleased with myself which I suspect I should not be feeling.

*What about?*

At being quick to realise the drawbacks and not being lulled into a false sense of contentment. I don't know if I should be pleased about this but I am.

*Well you paid the price for it didn't you? For not being pleased.*

Yes but I'm not sure if I should feel this emotion.

97

*Well if you out-pace it you'll know the answer won't you?*

My teacher was always so strict about being smug. I am wary of this. I have discovered that a lot of our mediums when they came to this world were exhausted and drained.

*By working too hard? Or by the very nature of the task?*

Both. Also that they have expressed regret at not taking enough time to have progressed individually themselves. Not all of them feel this way but the discerning ones do. They too have become aware of shortcomings.

*But you're not left alone very much, are you, if you're a medium? People always pulling on you.*

Yes but they realise they should have made time for personal progress. One of our friends said to me recently: 'I allowed myself to be kept at one level, and I should have pulled against it.'

*Yes, this is indeed a problem.*

They too have their problems.

§ Barbie says to me, 'Marie, so be warned, dear lady, this could happen to you.'

*Calling a spade a spade yes?*

Some have come over here expecting a pat on the back for the work they have done. They are most surprised when this doesn't happen. One who saw herself – I don't know whether to say this – one who saw herself as the *crème de la crème* was most annoyed to discover that there was no rush forward to thank her for the work she carried out.

*The work was good all the same.*

The work was excellent, the testimonials were true and accurate of her work but there's no preferential treatment. Your only reward is to be more aware of what is going on and I don't know if that's a reward.

*I'd like to know how far the mediumistic qualities help. You have talked about the other side of the picture but in the next life I would imagine that this particular talent has special benefits and advantages as well, bought very hard as it usually is.*

Yes, your awareness is already increased, much more than would be normal. You are also quick to grasp what is going on. Also your link with the spirit world which has already been there enables you to make higher contacts over here. It is the understanding, however, of what you are receiving that can be difficult.

*Do they expect rather a lot of you?*

More than the rest, yes. One is the teacher's bright pupil. Does this answer your question?

*Yes it does. Are there any 'green eyes' over there?*

Oh yes. This has not changed but after a time, once you become selfish like me, you haven't time and you outgrow this.

*I do so enjoy these talks.*

I do too.

*Like a good journalist you find a different angle.*

That's because of my training in the past.

*You mean in earlier lives?*

Some of it.

99

*Some of it? Do you go back beyond Greece to Egypt?*

Yes.

*Did we know one another then?*

Yes.

*It's very strange isn't it? I bet you've been a priest at some time.*

I was a scribe.

*A scribe . . . was that why Estelle called you John the Scribe?*

Yes.

*So there's more to that than met the eye?*

Yes.

*As so often. Do you go back to China?*

There is a vague something there. I have still to think on this.

*Do you get valuable lessons when you go back in memory?*

Oh yes. Unfortunately it is only over here that such things become clearer.

## EIGHTEEN

## 25TH SEPTEMBER 1985

I am beginning to feel a little bit more content with my progress.

*Ah that's good.*

But I remind myself that I must be wary of this contentment, for it would be too easy to relax one's yearning for knowledge, and become content.

*It's a familiar trap isn't it?*

One I fully intend to be wary of. I have had such a period before and was aware of what was happening. Nevertheless there are times when there is a feeling of euphoria which creeps over you, and can be most corrupting. I also find now that words are clumsy although words were my speciality. This is because telepathic communication is so much more satisfying, the nuances that one is able to convey by thought are so much more than can be achieved with clumsy words. I was always aware that this would be the case but not to such a degree as I am now. So, my friend, forgive me if I sometimes stumble, for when I am with you I am having to go back to this clumsy way of communication. I have tried to speak to the woman you have asked me to whom you never met, but unfortunately I was told in a very dignified way to go away and leave her alone. I do not want to risk making a nuisance of myself to her. I can only now wait and try and find another suitable period.

*Yes, well understood.*

She seems wrapped up in her own problems. Many come over in this state of mind and when they do they can exist in this state for some time. They turn inward and not outward. It is therefore then very difficult for those of us who would speak with them.

*Yes.*

We speak in your world of turning a deaf ear. In the level over here this can be done to a much greater degree. And so I'm afraid your lady is turning a deaf ear to my persuasion.

*Yes, well thank you very much for trying to help.*

I think the lady sees me as someone whom she doesn't know and who is interfering. Unfortunately there are people who come to this level of existence and who react to it in very different ways. Some blossom, some seem to shrivel as if it is all too much for them. This of course has never been my problem.

*No.*

The human spirit without the trappings of the physical world that it once belonged to can be very vulnerable, especially if those trappings became such a part of their life. I find this hard to put into words my friend.

*It's rather like a man whose business runs him instead of vice versa.*

Similar but not quite what I have tried to say.

*More subtle of course.*

102

I could think the thought at you telepathically, it would be so much easier, but again I will try to use words. Sometimes the trappings of this world become so entwined with the human spirit that when the human spirit is stripped away from them, or they are stripped away, the human spirit is lost and huddles within itself. Feeling rather like a new born child, very vulnerable and naked. Others delight in freedom. I think this explains it better.

*Yes.*

The difficulty is that one does not realise how this can be dealt with until one is faced with the problem. [§ He's cross. I've used the word 'one', and he doesn't like it.]

Many times I have seen the spirit of someone being dwarfed and dominated by the level of reality that they are able to understand. I have also seen others glory in the freedom. Definitely to have the gift of imagination is an advantage in this existence. Truly to think that all things are possible is to make all things possible. Sometimes my neat and tidy way of thinking abhors what it sees as untidiness and loose threads. I know there is a pattern, I have seen part of it and also had it explained, but it is such a loosely woven pattern that it seems to me at times to be in danger of unravelling. Of course I know this cannot be. Nevertheless my neat and tidy reasoning processes reel from what appears to be disorganised. The expression 'everyone does their own thing' that is so prevalent in your level, really applies to this one.

*In this subject there are a lot of musical instruments and everybody tends to play their own tune, perhaps can't do otherwise.*

This is true, I find great difficulty in this myself but I try carefully to remember and to be subjective, although this was something I also found difficult in your world.

§ He's having to search for words more. This is something new, he used not to have this problem.

*Well I think he's dealing with more difficult concepts.*

§ True, yes but usually he's very quick. But it could be.

## NINETEEN

## 13TH NOVEMBER 1985

§ Maurice Barbanell is shaking his head so I don't know if there's been some trouble recently – he's saying something about the world.

*Sounds like bad news.*

Every so often when I am in contact with this level the thoughts of hate, great confusion, turmoil, strike me afresh. I suppose that must be an improvement for me, I am becoming more aware of it. I cannot remember at the beginning being so aware. It's rather like hearing a lot of discordant music, all jangling away. I'm shaking my head because I find it hard to believe that I could live in amongst it and not be so aware of it. Certainly this sense of awareness seems to increase when the physical body is no longer around. I feel like someone who has been seeing the landscape, the countryside through a car window but not aware of the nuances of it. Now I've stepped out of the car and I am flooded with sound and sensations. I do not think even in our awareness we realised how constricting and confining the physical body was to the senses. My progress continues to move slowly.

*All the better for it being slow no doubt.*

Sometimes so slowly I wonder if there is any being made. I can only judge it at times like this, when I become

105

so much more aware of the strain that surrounds your level, which as I say I have never felt so strongly before. I wonder if it is getting worse? I suspect, my friend, it might be.

*You don't think it's only your increased sensitivity?*

I agree that may be a possibility, but it is equally possible that your level is becoming emotionally more confused and erratic in its behaviour.

## 4TH DECEMBER 1985

§ Three people are standing here, Paul. One is Maurice Barbanell. But he's got two ladies with him. One of the ladies looks like a photograph I've seen of Ena Twigg. Is she in spirit?

*Oh yes.*

§ You see I've never met Ena Twigg, I've never seen her in the flesh.

*Strange isn't it?*

§ This lady is not very tall and she's nodding her head so I think it must be. The other lady's taller, quite a commanding looking woman. Really a big woman and she says she's an old friend of yours and she's also a medium.

*Well naturally I can have a good guess.*

§ I asked her who she was and she answered me with a riddle. She said who would you expect Barbie to bring with him? Would you understand that?

*Yes. I mean I entirely agree with the commanding presence but I think of her as slim, or on the slim side.*

§ Yes but she's tall. And she's very commanding. When I said big, I didn't mean that way. I mean she's

107

much taller than me. This lady who is Ena Twigg seems possibly smaller than me, maybe about the same size, not much in it.

*That's right.*

§ But this woman is very much taller.

*There's no doubt in my mind who it is. Very nice to welcome them both.*

§ She's laughing. She says I don't know why we're here, I don't know why he brought us. Barbie said he thought you might want other opinions. The tall lady says he's very persuasive, he always has been. She says many's the time he used to talk her into things but she says it's nice to see you. We haven't spoken for a long time. She's laughing and making a joke about her and Barbie. She says Barbie and I have guides in common. Red Indians, and she's laughing.

*I see what she means, yes! Well I never thought of either of them as Red Indians really.*

§ She says that's why she's laughing, but they portrayed themselves as such.

*Has her guide really left the world for the time being?*

You'll hear little bits from him but basically yes.

*I see, yes.*

§ She has been in the position of Barbie, rather neglected by her guide since she came over. We have spoken now and again but not to the same degree. She says he laughed about the picture.

*What, the skotograph?*

§ She says he did it for evidence.

108

*I'd rather it had been a photograph of Yusepha-is.*

§ She's smiling. Yes, but would they have been ready for it? The one was more acceptable than the other.

*That's right.*

§ Ena Twigg – has a bird-like quality about her, very quick moving.

*That's right. Very quick.*

§ I hope I'm not offending her by saying that.

*Oh I don't think so. She's got too much sense.*

§ Anyway she's patted your shoulder in that quick way and she said listen, it is as we expected it, but our senses were not prepared for it.

*Do you mean it's more exacting than we think?*

§ Yes. I have spoken to the Archbishop she said, over here. She tells me that was his earth title.

*Yes. She's talking of one who was Archbishop a good many years ago?*

§ Yes. I have spoken to the Archbishop and he is of the opinion that religion blinkers one. He still feels bad about the report. Not just the damage he did to himself but the damage he did to others. He seemed a sad and rather lonely man when I spoke to him. Having difficulty adapting to a new way of thinking.

*Well there's certainly somebody that Barbie knew that would be able to help.*

§ Barbie just stepped forward, he said we've tried. His thoughts aren't flexible enough for this yet.

*Sad.*

I thought you would like to hear from the ladies.

*Yes indeed.*

§ Ena is taking me into a room, Paul, and there's things hanging on the wall but they're not photographs. Things framed on the walls. She's telling me she had a room like this.

*Yes, it was a rather crowded room.*

§ She says testimonials.

*That's right.*

§ A lot of knick-knacks in it as well.

*She had things that she valued, that people had given her.*

§ Yes, that's right but it's crowded. It's almost like a sort of trophy room. Alright. She tells me she doesn't remember much about her passing.

*No, that's good.*

§ She expected to be aware of it but it was very confusing at the end. She wanted to be aware of every minute of it but she wasn't. The one thing she can remember is a peculiar lightness, as if she had no weight. She's with her husband.

*Oh yes.*

§ She describes him as a very patient man.

*Yes he was indeed.*

§ He was always in the background. Many people didn't know I had a husband.

*I wouldn't have thought it because he went everywhere with her.*

§ Yes but he had a habit of keeping well in the background.

*That's completely true.*

§ He wouldn't always sit beside me, he would sit somewhere else.

*That's right. Did Harry help her over the passing?*

§ He was very good, he joked all the time and kept telling me I should have no problem. He was an angel. I did so enjoy our chats although we didn't always agree.

*No we didn't, but we both cared about what we were talking about. That was important.*

§ That was what was stimulating. She pulled back from public work. This was something you didn't agree with. Not at first.

*No I don't think that was so. Perhaps I was a bit politic.*

§ She's speaking of a daughter. I am most distressed; she seems to have pulled away from certain things. It's not that she doesn't believe. Could you understand this?

*Yes perfectly.*

§ It's not that she doesn't believe but she doesn't want to be involved.

*That's absolutely right.*

§ I'm so unhappy for here because she's missing out. She could be doing so well.

*Well perhaps she's doing well in another setting.*

§ She's talking about being more interested in her home life, as if that is where her energies are going. Maybe she had too much of psychic things.

*Could be.*

§ And this is the reaction. I will not try to influence her.

*No that's right.*

§ I didn't here and I won't do it from spirit although at one time I was not as wise. Anyway she's smiling, she says she's more her father's daughter.

*And like him a hard worker.*

§ Yes and for the home, rather than the world that I worked with. I was aware that I was in your thoughts. We seem to have known each other such a long time.

*Yes much longer than we think, or than I think.*

§ I'm sorry to see what is happening.

*We're all sorry and it's very hard to know how to remedy it.*

§ Yes, we have spoken of this over here.

*Where do you make an impact? That's the problem, however small.*

§ Through books, good mediums. The world you're living in is looking for something.

*Oh yes indeed.*

§ More now than ever before. Maybe all the lights will join up and become one big one. I do know this, old friend, neither of us can give up.

*No.*

§ The tall lady is now speaking. She says thank you for remembering me.

*Oh what could be easier?*

§ She remembers you as a very serious young man.

*That's quite right.*

§ That is the way you always struck her. She's a very elegant lady.

*Looked very nice on the platform.*

§ She's got style. She's laughing, she didn't see why you needed to look dowdy on the platform! So many of us are over here now.

*Yes. Do you plan to work together or have you gone your own separate ways as they say?*

§ Too individual for that. We could never do it in this world, how can we do it here? She's laughing at the idea.

*Well if they all put in their separate oar in some place or other it might make an impact gradually.*

§ Oh we all wish your world well and we would do our utmost to help. After all having worked for spirit in your world, the habit is hard to die. I do not see the respect for our young colleagues in your world, the way it used to be. Have you noticed?

*It's true, this is a young generation without respect, it has other qualities.*

§ I used to get respect more than those who are now in your world.

*Well then you had a very special place.*

§ Yes but where there is respect there is also the earning of that respect. Which comes first?

113

*Well the earning of it comes first doesn't it? But maybe something else is preferred to be earned. Some might feel they gain more by being free and easy.*

§ This is possibly true but nevertheless I notice this.

*But then you had a very unusual degree of accuracy on the platform and that brought respect didn't it?*

§ I was fortunate in that I worked during a serious period in peoples lives. Therefore no one came without serious intent. There was none of the attitude that is in your world now, a lightheartedness towards the subject. I could say that people genuinely wanted proof and wanted to know.

*Well people today want to find out more by themselves rather than from other people.*

§ They want advice how to guide their lives. They would draw my colleagues in your world down to the status of a fortune teller.

*That's all too true.*

§ No one wanted that in my day. We were a more serious generation with more serious things in the conditions around us.

*Do you have a team?*

§ Slowly we are gathering. Our objective is something we have to agree upon. We have so many ideas, so many things we want to do. It is harnessing all to the one goal.

*You've got to do it without too much help from the boss?*

§ All this part, the boss says, we must do ourselves. Being in spirit as we are, he says, we no longer need

114

that type of help. It was different when we were there. I always remember when we first met. Can you?

*Certainly. I was in trouble and you helped. I couldn't forget that could I?*

§ I remember how sad you were, how confused. And by the time we met again you were very much involved in this.

*Yes that's right.*

§ And I was pleased. She said to give you love from Mrs Roberts. Would you understand?

*It's just a little bit of evidence, Marie, to clinch.*

§ Barbanell says, 'I told you I wouldn't get a word in.'

## TWENTY

## 19TH FEBRUARY 1986

§ He says – I've not to say 'He says' – 'It's good to see you, my friend. The Old Fellow says the more people understand the more they come closer to us.' He added that the Old Fellow was always a practical man.

But only those who really studied the man understood that. Others would not have said so. Many of our former colleagues from your level that are now here, are also interested. You have got us talking about how all this should be presented. Your new book is on such a vast subject. I tried to do this myself once, it didn't come off very well. I was better when I was letting spirit write the books. I think it was my personality. I tended to make the facts fit what I believed. A common fault.

To be a true observer one must leave self out. It is nice when you come against facts which confirm your own feelings on a subject but it can also be a trap, for you then tend to fit square pegs into round holes and hammer them in to make them fit. I think my own abilities as a medium got in the way, and my own personal experiences.

*Your particular became your general too.*

Yes. You follow me. You may come against contradictions.

*I'm bound to, yes.*

116

But the exception can be the rule also. You will be better, my friend, forgive me, because you are older and age brings more observation, the passion has gone, and observation is left. There is an impartiality, an objectivity, that one can bring but I was not able to do so. I am continually testing my pre-conceived ideas. There is still the danger of creating my own reality, although I am on my guard against this. If only one's awareness could be a piece of elastic.

*You mean going up and down levels of consciousness?*

Yes. Mine is not as elastic as I would require.

*But at least you haven't got to put out an established point of view every week, as you did here.*

I think that was bad training for this level.

*I think it was.*

I became accustomed to guidelines, to a parameter of thought. Now my horizons must be as wide as possible and I am constantly defeating myself in this.

*Defeating yourself? How so?*

By pre-judging, by trying to assemble things too quickly into a neat pattern because I am used to working in this way, and not letting it make its own pattern.

*Yes but time is on your side now and not against it.*

When was I ever a patient man? Even my best friends would never have said this of me.

*No, but you had certain sides of patience very well actually.*

But the hunger is more here. You feel you are missing out on so much. I don't think I can describe it, you would

117

have to experince it. You know the glimpses we all have, my friend? Where suddenly everything seems to fit but they do not last, these glimpses. Well they come more often here, these glimpses of perfection, of order within chaos, of a completeness about everything. It can be very frustrating. To be blind over here can sometimes be a blessing.

*Temporarily?*

Yes. As you can see my identity is still as strong as ever. I seem to remember a period when I worried about this. It no longer is a worry. So much of our identity comes from those around us.

*As you have said before.*

And there comes a period when you seem to exist only as people see you and in your relationship to them, almost as if you wouldn't be there at all unless you were there for them. But this has all gone now. I do not know if it was a crisis but it felt like one. I cannot say I have felt elated that that hurdle is now behind me. I seem to have passed it without realising when I passed it.

*That seems to happen a lot on your side.*

All the time. It's only in retrospect you understand. Now I have the wish to be a piece of elastic and so I think another crisis is looming.

*It's a humble ambition isn't it?*

No, no, at the moment it seems an immense ambition.

*Then it must be a very big bit of elastic.*

Limitless.

I see our common friend's health has not been too good. He seems to be taking a back seat now, almost as if

118

he's withdrawing into himself. Even you must have noticed this?

*Maybe he's meditating more.*

Yes but it is more than this.

*Then what's the positive aspect for him?*

To start assembling what he has learned, to meditate, to review. To start sifting through the many experiences and formulating his thoughts, his ideas, his awareness and his knowledge. There is time for that.

*This is for his benefit rather than for the benefit of the world?*

Yes. He is not too interested in the world now. He tries to be but he is not.

*Has he ever been a monk in an earlier life or a holy man of some sort?*

Yes, of course. His spirit is saying I have done that bit, now I want to do this bit. He is becoming contemplative. You will find his interest not easily roused, although he tries for your sake. Each of us prepares for the next level in different ways, this is his way.

*Well it's a good way isn't it? A very good way.*

For him yes, for you no. For you clarify yourself best by writing. I do not know if you have noticed this?

*Well I suppose it's part of the discipline of writing.*

It makes you sort things out.

*That's true.*

I think if you had to do it his way you would put if off, or say 'Later I will have time for this', but the way you are

119

doing it, you are tackling it now. Always you will find in your writings that there is more knowledge there than you realised you had. Sometimes I know you think not enough but also sometimes you are surprised.

*I don't know how it comes about.*

That you surprise yourself?

*Yes.*

Some is from the help of the one you know who helps you, but some is from your own spirit, all the time it is sifting, retaining some things, letting others go. I cannot say I have noticed a vast change in my spirit awareness. I expected there to be vast changes. Yet if I compare what I know and am aware of now with what I knew and was aware of then, there is a difference, but the difference seems to be that the subconscious has joined with the conscious. You understand?

*Yes, pretty well.*

And so I am different from then, but also not different.

*You've come together?*

Yes and I wonder how much more has to come. I remember once being told, and you were too, that all we needed was already known to our spirit. I accepted it without really understanding it, but I think I understand it better now. It's to do with seeing through a glass darkly. Looking back it seems that at times I have spoken to you rather pessimistically. Now I am much more optimistic.

*Well I suppose you had expectations that weren't altogether fulfilled at first?*

I think this is probably true. It is not just the young who think they know everything. I had prided myself on being

120

aware and knowledgeable because of what spirit had taught me but I realise now I had only scratched the surface.

I have seen Myers.

*What is there between you, apart from general interest?*

He thinks we may have got our information from the same source.

*That's not unlikely is it?*

But no one is admitting this to us. We have to reach this ourselves.

*So this has brought him into fellowship with you?*

Not quite fellowship, he is a difficult man still. Not always comfortable to be with. His mind reminds me of a firework, one never knows when it is going to explode. Sometimes I think I have kept up with him and then he's lost me. He hasn't changed. I felt a little bit guilty because I had not really read his books. You knew this?

*It doesn't surprise me. I didn't of course know you felt guilty.*

Only when we speak of them and I realise the effort he put into them to try and explain. I skimmed through a little bit but never properly read. I hope others will not do as I have done, for the man's passion and sincerity cannot be overlooked. He makes me feel quite dull, he is so cxcited.

*At new things?*

Yes, and fitting others into place. I'm afraid I can only sustain conversation with him for a little period and then he loses me again. I do try to maintain the contact because there are glimmerings there of understanding that I am beginning to reach. He asked me why I came to see you

121

personally. He says I still have not understood. I'm telling
him I don't understand what he's talking about. You see I
put all of myself here. I started to say it was for the
medium's sake and he said no, it was because I still
thought in those terms. He says my time and space
thinking is still of earth level. I think he is right. You can
understand how difficult it is to sustain a conversation like
this.

*Indeed yes.*

I feel I'm almost grasping, but not quite, what he is
speaking of. He's such a serious man. He makes me feel
almost shallow in comparison. I thought you would be
interested to hear of the meeting.

*Very, very interested indeed.*

I try to remember these things when I come. That's why
I think I should have read more of the books, maybe I
would have understood him then, and not appeared such
an idiot.

*But Myers obviously has a mind that's both quick silver
and on fire, it's a difficult combination.*

That's why I said a firework. He takes leaps with his
mind and I cannot follow him over the gulf. I can follow
where there is my type of logic and reasoning, his seems
to me at times blind leaps into the dark and yet something
within me knows he's right. That's why I need my elastic.
Sylvia has withdrawn. She too is meditating. Also I am
worried about the link between the spirit and the physical;
Sylvia is becoming very weak.

*Yes. Does that matter so much?*

Confusion is setting in.

122

*Old people get confused; it's understood. You were spared that.*

Yes and I would wish she had been spared it also for in the past she had such commonsense.

*She even used to haul you over the coals now and again.*

It was good, she kept my feet on the ground. I think that was her greatest gift to all of us, her commonsense, her down to earthness and her joy in life.

*Yes. And she always kept her commonsense available didn't she, in whatever field she was talking about?*

She would listen so patiently to others and then gently point out when they were going off in tangents. No, leave her be.

§ He's much more cheerful today, Paul. I wouldn't say bubbling over but it's like a different person. He's bouncy.

*He's obviously moved on a stage hasn't he?*

§ Yes and yet it seems he hasn't from what he's saying, yet I can see the difference. I mean this throwing back his head and laughing and joking, it's never been so apparent before. Almost as if there's not so much pressure.

*Yes but you've also got a very good link today haven't you?*

The medium is improving.

*Now it's your turn to laugh, Marie.*

She's even using some of my big words which I wouldn't have had the confidence to give her earlier.

123

*As between you and him, Marie, you've improved the situation by a mutual generosity.*

She has stopped disliking me because I ignored her when she was a young medium. [§ And he's laughing.]

*Well the laugh is on him really isn't it?*

§ Yes. I, Marie, have worked hard and in a way it has been good that I was ignored by him as a young medium because I have had to work all by myself and learn my own way.

I might not really have done her a favour by discovering her.

*You might have made it too easy for her? Then that wouldn't have been good.*

At an impressionable stage. [§ He is smiling and saying, 'I still have the last word, you see.']

## TWENTY-ONE

# 7TH MARCH 1986

*In the first part of this interview the medium had tried to assist an unskilled and emotionally confused communicator.*

Sorry, old friend, tried to help.

*It's very nice of you because I know it's not a job you really much like.*

I don't like it at all but felt I owed it to you and the medium. Have seen too many things like this in the past happening. People coming before they're ready. Have seen people in the world I used to be in being clumsy in handling a spirit message, now I'm seeing the other side of the coin. Don't want to work too hard with this medium now. She has a bit of a headache from trying to hold on to that woman. Shouldn't have done it, I would have stopped her.

*Well it was her good conscience that made her hang on wasn't it?*

Being selfish, because the result is that now I can't talk properly.

*Well you'll have another chance soon.*

Anyway you must be fed up speaking to me. [§ He's laughing again.]

125

*Not at all. I take a lot of feeding in this direction.*

I'm glad to hear it.

*I'm sometimes waiting for the main course to come on.*

So am I. I'm close, very close, I think. The trouble is it seems to me you get more help on your level than you do on this one.

*That's a bit cryptic.*

The Old Fellow says go and find out.

*That's like him isn't it?*

Says I don't need so much help now and so I spend a lot of my time renewing old acquaintances.

*On your side?*

Yes.

*Like a Pied Piper?*

To a certain extent but also picking crumbs.

*What do you need with crumbs?*

Some have been over here much longer than me. Occasionally it works, I learn a bit more. It's so important to open all the doors, I mean in me, not in the world I'm in.

*Have you talked to Conan Doyle about this?*

Yes and others. I'm trying to pick their brains. Some are like me, some are more lethargic, some think I'm trying to rush things but I was never a patient man when it came to knowledge.

*No.*

126

I know there are those who think I'm trying to do it too fast. I don't think so, *I* don't think so.

*I expect you're a good judge of your own pace really.*

Such a hunger, but I am learning, I am growing, I think. Don't think I'll ever make a guide.

*Why not?*

Would have no patience with that woman.

*Well maybe she wouldn't be one of your charges.*

If I worked for a medium, she would be. Don't think I would be acceptable for the job anyway, ordering them away to sort themselves out.

*Good in the long run.*

[§ He's laughing.] Would be sad for the medium.

## TWENTY-TWO

## 19TH MARCH 1986

I'm glad we're getting this opportunity to speak. I was going to comment on the length of time since we last spoke but I am finding this increasingly difficult to do.

*Oh a very short while, only a week or so.*

Ah, I wasn't sure. I was always so time-conscious in your world. It's a little bit difficult at times to accept the timelessness where I am. One feels a little bit disorientated at first. You don't realise when you're on your level how much you relate to time even in your manner of speech.

I feel I'm making more improvement. It's like chasing the missing bits of a jigsaw puzzle. Sometimes you see things from such a distance, I mean emotional distance, that you feel your humanity slipping. Can you understand this?

*Yes, I can a bit.*

As if the doings of the people in your world are rather like some ritual dance. You are one of the few people I can speak to in this way. At times this has worried me – there, I use the word time again, you see what I mean?

*Yes, yes.*

I feel: is this the right way to go, should I be viewing from the distance?

*I suppose it's all preparation for when you'll disappear for the time being? See I'm using time now!*

What about the love, the caring you and I have experienced from the spirit world on this level? Where does that come in as you view more from the distance? You can understand my dilemma? I have spoken to others over this and some have said I have to appreciate and understand the pattern first, then you regain what you might call the human touch. I spoke once to you before about the distance I felt was increasing between my relatives and myself.

*Yes you did.*

I am aware now more than ever how much we personalise our relationships on your level. We talk about a meeting of souls and soul links, but only when you're over here do you start to understand it properly. Words are so difficult. I would like to give you a bundle of my thoughts and have you sort them out. I listen to myself speaking to you and what I want to say is so fragmented. It's as if over here I find myself going more into myself. Not worrying about relating to others, but relating to me. This is very difficult. So many times I am on the point of exclaiming 'Ah, now I have it' – and it eludes me. My concepts keep changing. Sometimes I feel lost among my own thoughts. This is not an unhappy state of being but a confusing one.

*It's like a reverie I suppose in a way.*

No, more than that. I keep waiting for something clicking and everything falling neatly into the pattern. I feel there is a nucleus of me that I have to reach, that I have layers to go through yet.

*Part of what you've derived from experiences in other lives do you think?*

I suspect so. I feel I have to strip away these layers. I feel I have the key but don't know where the lock is. Sometimes I talk with others whom I judge can be and are on a higher awareness level. It can be very frustrating to talk to such people.

*Why is that?*

The tantalising glimpses they give you of understanding. I think I can understand one bit, but another bit eludes me – yet they must link. That other Paul was right when he spoke of seeing through a glass darkly. Sometimes I feel elation. Sometimes I feel frustration. This is not to say that there are others over here who feel this also, some do, some are quite content with what they have. In this way it is very much like our world. I do know the answer lies within myself rather than as an outward experience. I am beginning to accept the fact that when I am feeling like this there is a new stage of growth coming for me. Whereas when I am happy, or at least content, there is danger that I'm standing still. Although there are those who will help and with whom you can spend so much time, always it comes back to you, and how much you can absorb.

*I don't understand what really makes the growth process over there.*

I think it is what I am going through now, my friend. It is like giving birth to an idea, to a concept, to a new way of thinking. Try to imagine it as stepping stones across a river and each stepping stone a new way of looking, a new angle of thinking. As you reach each one, slowly you move over to the other side of the river, only here you move onwards. I look back at the religions of the world that I have left and I suspect that the Buddhist Nirvana has the most similarity to what I am experiencing over here. I say I suspect because I do not know, but this divorcing yourself from personal love and friendships, this seeing the pattern – I believe the Buddha tried to come the closest to explaining. Whereas with Christianity it was too simplistic. You understand? To see yourself as part of a whole is difficult, yet again I suspect that is what I'm aiming towards and you have thought this also.

*Yes.*

It is easy to say, but to actually get down to the reality of it is different. Now this ties in with Buddhist belief of being part of everything. The Nirvana they spoke of. Yet it seems to demand that I have to become more knowledgeable of myself first, as if I must sweep away layers that have accumulated over a long period of time.

*Over many lives you mean?*

Yes. I have had to leave your world with the knowledge and awareness I had gained to come to this level, with this knowledge and awareness to sweep away the layers. Am I making sense? I have thought about how I would try to explain this to you. Oh it is very exciting!

*Oh yes.*

But the frustration is finding the handle, the handle to use.

*When you've found the handle and it all comes into a whole do you reckon then that'll be the time you will disappear from our contacts for the time being?*

I'm not sure. It is possible. I think if I could answer your question I would have the handle but whether this will lead only to another set of questions . . .

*Bound to surely.*

131

. . . and another handle that I'm looking for I don't know. Still it doesn't get boring.

*I can see some readers scratching their heads if they read this.*

I wish I could put it in simple words. I'm trying very hard to do so. Can we tell them that to cling to relationships once they are in spirit is wrong, that one must move back from this and move on, that these are souls you have only temporarily linked with, that you may have nothing in common with? Can we speak of these things and they would understand?

*I don't think they would accept it.*

Yet you know I am right. This is why I have spoken of the Buddhist theory and also what our Old Gentleman tried to say. You understand? Personal relationships hold us back from advancement for they are of your level. I think he who said we are all brothers and sisters of God was using a simplistic term to explain this. Some say, over here, that my humanity will come back when I love all. At the moment I have been worried about losing the love I have for people that I already love.

*Is it not only the opposite end of the pendulum you're working at now?*

Yes, this is my problem.

*At the centre point perhaps both will be true in some way we can't quite understand.*

Let us take so simple a thing as my concern for Sylvia. At first I have been very concerned, now the concern is not there. I see only her soul's progress and view it from the distance, yet I am reluctant to give up this love I have felt. You see my problem?

132

*Yes I do.*

Has no one else ever spoken of this to you, my friend?

*Not quite like this, no.*

Somehow I felt such love would remain always constant, especially in the case of people who would be like Sylvia and myself. This is what I mean by viewing from the distance.

*Will there not be relationship at a deeper level, impersonal somehow but very real?*

This is possible.

*Members of a group?*

This I think could well be but it's very difficult to accept, or believe in at this stage.

*I suppose you had to leave go in order to take hold again at a different level?*

This is what someone said to me over here. Strangely enough someone you know.

*Really? Are you going to tell me who or not?*

Let us see if you can guess who would speak this way to me.

*My teacher, Peter?*

Yes.

*Is that right?*

Yes. He said, 'You are clinging to a relationship in the way you clung to it in the earth world, but you are no longer in that world and so all things change and go further. You are stepping back to see more clearly.' He said I was looking at Sylvia with human eyes, not spirit

133

eyes and trying to retain the love on that level. I think you are understanding my problems?

*A bit I think.*

Well you too will have it.

*I feel it rather than understand it.*

I am trying to understand it. In my limited understanding it seems to me I have to alter my way of thinking and feeling about Sylvia and the others that I love. In doing so it seems I would be breaking certain ties, or bonds that tie me to one way of thinking, even to a behaviour pattern.

*Are you not getting ready to see the deeper Sylvia?*

I see her as a soul struggling. The old me would have been in there helping, using all I could to help, but there is a distance now as if I view her soul struggle and know it must be, that we are not two people closely bound together but two individuals with their own soul's path to go and that I mustn't interfere but accept this pattern. It's as if I'm transported back to the period before we knew each other. As you know with a marriage partner this is very difficult.

*Yes.*

For you start to feel as one and now I have to feel as two again. Oh, no one makes me do this, this is something that in my quest for knowledge and understanding has developed, and there is within me a feeling of rejection of it. Yet, like you, I seem to know that it is part of my progression.

*And inevitable.*

At one stage or another, whether now or later, yes, for

134

I know her soul also experiences this. I think now I am beginning to really understand the meaning of soul mate but not in the terms it has ever been used before. I often think we must still be on a similar level.

*You and Sylvia?*

No, you and I for I find that most of the time you understand what I am speaking of, but then you have Peter, I should expect this.

*Plenty of puzzles there, eh?*

I asked him whether I should discuss this with you and he said, 'Yes – he needs stretching.' He also asked me why I worried about being alone.

*What did you reply?*

That I didn't know I worried about it. He said, 'But you do, you are trying to stay with old relationships, with old loves.' He added, 'This is why those who would achieve spirituality, awareness in our world, had, in your world, to walk alone and be alone.' In other words again, distancing themselves from personal relationships. He said they did it there on earth, you're having to learn this thing here. He said he was surprised that I had not noticed the significance of this among those we had had on the earth plane refusing to be involved in very personal relationships.

*Well, White Eagle has many loving relationships with those on earth.*

He would say, he has loving relationships with anyone who comes to him. He would say all people but not particularly personalised. I know, I had already asked him this question.

*You had? You seem amused?*

135

Yes because you thought of this question also. I will struggle on. Nevertheless because he said it would do you no harm to know of my struggle I have brought it to you.

*Thank you, I appreciate it.*

But there is a reluctance to give this up, a strong reluctance, almost one feels rebellious, rebelling against it.

*Yes, yet you can't.*

Oh, I have been told I always had a choice. I said to Peter, 'So this is what is demanded of me for my future role.' And he said, 'No one demands anything of you, you make these demands on yourself.'

*So if you went back to the old it wouldn't satisfy you any more in the old way?*

No, it would not.

*That's the sadness of it in a way.*

I would begin to resent the love and feel it was changing me, yet I would be the one putting the chains on. It is difficult. Now I have given you enough of my worries. How are yours? Can I be of assistance to you?

*Would I be right in supposing that the present intention of those who come to us as guides and work in this field – call it Spiritualistic – are really trying to make us on earth see how things are much more serious in the spirit world so that gradually we can become the same on earth, or something of the same?*

Yes, although Peter and my friend would object to the word serious, as they have never behaved in a too serious fashion with us. Let us say they wish us to understand the aspect of growth, the urgency of growth, and they sugar the pill.

136

*So they're not too serious because they see us still as children, and they play accordingly?*

It is like you making a small game of a lesson you're teaching a child. To know what I am beginning to understand, you have already admitted would hurt many people in your world, and especially those who used to be my readers. Some would reject it because they do not want it to be this way.

*So it's well surely to utter it though, both for those and for other types of readers?*

Yes. We must, and for those who do not accept it and say, 'No, it will be lovely over there, I will be so happy', this is true, they will be but for the others who see beyond this stage, we must speak for their sake. But how do you sugar a pill that says the relationships you have with those you love as you know it now, will cease to be when you start to grow and can give them no promise it will return later? I do not think we will be very popular.

*I think not.*

I have given you a problem, my friend.

*Yes.*

I will leave you to think about it.

*I often say I'll write down one or two things just as I draw the coffin lid over me.*

It's the safest way. [§ He's laughing now.]

*I just thank him deeply for what he's said.*

I'm only carrying out Peter's instructions.

§ He really came very very deeply in. It was as if it was so serious he wanted me as far out of the way as he

137

could get me. I had the feeling that he thought what he was going to say would disturb me. As if, if she knows too much of what I'm going to say she's going to start interfering, changing it, watering it down, whatever.

*But you didn't.*

§ It quite stunned me, what he said today.

## TWENTY-THREE

## 24TH APRIL 1986

§ Barbanell's been standing back like an observer.

*Well I expect he's been doing some hard work behind the scenes just the same.*

§ He said just now, 'I'm glad I didn't do your type of mediumship.'

*I don't think he'd have had the patience you know.*

§ He threw back his head and laughed, in the way you'd laugh if someone hit the nail on the head.

I look from this level and where our Movement once widened out the reverse is happening. There will be those who think this is a bad thing. However this was long overdue. We were beginning to ramble and speak with different voices. Not so in the initial stages but over this last period there have definitely been different voices.

I spoke to Rossiter recently and he agreed with me. Changes are taking place in all of these organisations, things will scatter a bit further yet and in that scattering become vague and unspecified. Do not despair, for the nucleus will remain untouched and can begin again. Already you have been aware of things and of seeing things that have distressed you.

*Yes.*

As it would have done me in your place. Still be of good heart, the bush will be pruned back to become more sturdy. The distress that you have experienced and felt, Rossiter says to tell you he has been through this already in the past. You never knew each other very well.

*No.*

I was surprised to learn you only met each other on a few occasions. Somehow I supposed you had known each other better than that.

*No.*

I had just presumed that there was more knowledge of each other. Unfortunately your level is becoming more and more gimmicky and this is creeping in everywhere. He wished you to know he understood your sadness.

*Good, that's kind of him.*

But did not wish you to give up hope as we both believe and know it must get worse before it can then revert back again. The mediums will survive. When all is said and done, spirits of the mediums will again instruct. I must say I am now glad I am where I am for though I can be dispassionate now, this would not have been so, and I fear I would have encouraged you to rebel. I do not know if you would have listened.

*It's natural to me to rebel.*

But I think you would have.

*Now I've got to be careful not to.*

For they would only remember the rebellion and not what came before. Use what you have spoken of, but it will not be overshadowed by rebellion, which could happen if you took another course.

*Yes. I'm glad he's reinforced me in this.*

I still admit I would think differently there in your world but my time sense is now different and I know the mediums will survive to straighten out that which has become crooked, to return again to what you and I both know. And so it will almost return to the way it started, but not quite, but do not be distressed about this, my friend.

*Right.*

PART II

## TWENTY-FOUR

## 4TH JUNE 1986

*I'm feeling, rightly or wrongly, that the time's quite close when you are going to disappear from our immediate ken and if this is so I'm wondering if you would like to give a kind of resumé of your path since you died, and where it is different from how the Spiritualists as a rule expect it to be and so that it could be a kind of message to them. How do you react to that?*

§ He's smiling and he's shrugging his shoulders but says he's game to try.

*Good, fine.*

Regarding moving on, it's possible you could be right that we are reaching a period where it will no longer be so easy to communicate with you in this way. I am still finding it hard to judge my progress but from little signs that I am experiencing, I feel that there are some changes taking place. You know, however, even if this does take place I will try to find another method of communicating.

*Ah good.*

Whether it will be possible to do I cannot say. And so I take it you wish me to start the resumé now?

*If you're ready; otherwise say what you came to say, it makes no difference.*

No, I knew you had this idea in mind and so prepared myself slightly for it.

*In fact you're a blooming thought-reader, yes?*

Where shall we start? Do you want it from the moment of my passing?

*Yes please.*

I do not know if this will be a garbled account or confused because at the moment of my passing there were several things taking place at once. There was a sense of sinking, a feeling of bright light and I used this word deliberately, I couldn't see it but I felt it. This is what I mean about it being a garbled account. There was also the sensation of rising which sounds ridiculous when I already said I felt I was sinking. I can only look back and think this was the separating of the two parts, and so I was aware of both at the same time. I was conscious of some people clustered around the bed and the sensation was similar to the feelings one had when you received gas in the old days to get your teeth out. There is that sensation of coming to and a cluster of faces round you, only I was not told to spit in the bowl! It is the best way I can picture it for you. And similarly there was this sense of being disoriented. A feeling of not being quite awake because I could hear myself being discussed, yet I would be puzzled how to answer you if you said did I physically hear or hear in my head.

*These were people on the other side already, were they?*

Yes. Two I recognised as old friends that you and I both know – two men. One was Mother and strangely enough one was an uncle that I didn't have much to do with or know much about, but somehow I recognised him. I must admit to a feeling of disappointment because I expected

146

to see my guide but I was informed that this was not part of his duties, that he was there and aware of my passing but that those who had known me physically in this world were used at this stage to help me adjust. What I did then I am not sure of, there seem to be gaps in my memory. I suspect I floated between two states: at periods I was aware, at periods I seemed to be dreaming. Looking back, this does not seem to have lasted very long because suddenly I was awake and conscious, almost as if someone had snapped their fingers and suddenly I was there.

*You were yourself again as it were?*

Yes. How long this period lasted I do not know. I remember at one stage during this period thinking I must remember this and speak of it to others left behind but it was very difficult to be scientific about it while one was taking part in it.

*Were you surprised to go over just then?*

There was no pain. I have asked others since that period and you would be surprised at the number of people who have spoken of having no pain. Most experienced the same symptoms as myself, which was a lassitude, a tremendous weariness, a feeling of weakness – the expression weak as a kitten comes to mind. Now I understand why sleep is called the little death, very similar. No, I was not surprised at my passing, it was as if the other me knew it was taking place and immediately took over when the process started. There was also a strange sense of *déjà vu*. I felt I had done it before and knew the process that was taking place. I think I remembered other passings at that point. Certainly this inner me, the essence, the soul, the spirit, knew all along what was taking place and at this conscious me, the physical, was surprised I was not aware of it, almost as if

147

the subconscious took over the conscious. Am I clear?

*Yes, pretty clear.*

I am trying to be as precise as possible for you. It is difficult to describe and I find words so clumsy now.

This medium is having trouble with me because sometimes I send her thoughts rather than give her the words, this is why she keeps saying to me 'Say it again'.

There was the usual reunion then with others, and the pleasure of knowing that everything was similar to what I had expected. It was some while before I realised that therein lay the danger and I started questioning myself. Was I seeing what I wanted to see? But this came later. At first there was the joy of reunion. And the worry over those left behind, especially my wife and one friend who had been seriously ill also, whom I had been concerned about. Looking back that period seemed to me an idyllic period; no one spoke of anything but the pleasure at seeing me again and of course you know how I love to talk. I cannot time this period as you can understand, only that it existed. Physically I was aware of never feeling so good, I had never felt so good before, there was almost a state of ecstasy, a feeling of 'I've made it', which continued to remain with me for some time. At this same period I do not know if I went looking for my guide or he came looking for me but we met. We spoke for a period; what I can remember of what he said, is his advice to take my time adjusting, not to try and experience too much too quickly, and he told me finally that for a period he would be there if I needed him.

*Did he appear as the portrait or did he appear otherwise?*

He appeared otherwise and at first I did not recognise him but once he spoke it was like meeting someone who was familiar, yet not familiar. I told him that I had

148

expected to see him as he had shown himself to me in your world, but he said that would encourage me to remain on that level of thinking, that it was time to move on and to start experiencing reality, the reality of myself and the reality of my surroundings. I remember doing a lot of talking with those I had known before. Physically my surroundings seemed all that one would want.

*Did you create them or were they created for you?*

At this period I had not started to ask these questions. Later I discovered it was a combination of the two, of what I wanted to see, and of what they thought would help me adjust. I found it difficult at that period to get used to the timelessness of it. You would be surprised, my friend, how much that bothers you at first, although you think it wouldn't. Slowly my curiosity, which is never far from the surface, began to make me ask questions, and I found among my relatives those who were quite content to remain as they were, and so they could not answer my questions. At this period I found more help from our colleagues, the ones we had worked with and known in the past but again there was a difference; there were some who could answer my questions and some who had not even thought of them yet. At this point I found myself reviewing my life. This was not an easy period, this was my first uncomfortable period.

*Yes. Did you see it forwards or backwards?*

I saw it as a pattern.

*So it wasn't like a cinema reel, it was more like a mental process?*

It was a combination of the two. It was like those railways you have as a child where you watch the trains going in and around all the different tracks, cutting back,

149

going forward, only it was me I was watching rather than a train. Does this help?

*Yes, so it was a recapitulation rather than just a time track?*

Total, and every so often certain events would stand out where I had to make decisions or where there had been a crisis. Some of those I was not proud of. I had not thought myself vain or proud yet there were quite outstanding instances of this as I reviewed. I watched myself turn a deaf ear when I should have listened. I started questioning my motives. At first I made excuses for myself, 'What else could I do given the conditions at the time?' Sometimes I stopped because something embarrassed me or hurt me but I felt impelled back to look and see again. No one did this to me, yet it was like looking at my life in a miniature model of it. It is hard to describe. It wasn't like a cinema reel because I wasn't viewing this bit, then that bit, and then the next, but all of it at one point.

*So you saw the whole railway system at the same time?*

Yes. This is why in my description to you I have felt that I have had to call it a pattern rather than a reel because a reel implies that there is a beginning and an end, or an end and a beginning and you go from one to the other but this was all at the one period. And I realise now looking back that you have to see it in this fashion, there was something right about seeing it in that way.

*Would you say everybody does it this way or is this appropriate to your particular knowledge and condition?*

I would say everybody eventually has to do that; whether they do it at once, I am not sure. Then of course I started questioning myself. As I say, this was a difficult

150

period for me. Even now I feel that there are certain things I have not got to the bottom of regarding my own temperament, my own weaknesses. During this period the state of ecstasy seemed to diminish, it was still there but not so paramount. After this period the questions started coming more frequently, then I questioned the reality of what I was seeing, and my perception of it altered. I noticed that there were people who tended to group together, that there were others whom I called loners, who seemed to be going through a period similar to myself. I found that with relatives and people whom I had known in this world, we were no longer talking the same language to each other. Not that there was anything wrong with them but I had started to change, rather like saying to people, 'Did you see that, or what do you think of this?' and they don't know what you're talking about. And so, still caring, still loving, we seem to go our separate ways. During this period I seemed to spend a lot of time seeking those who could answer some of my questions. Of course there was the one who had been my guide. I also spoke with another, the one you and I both know but you know him better than I.

*Peter?*

Yes, and there were others who were a little bit ahead of me and who gave me some comfort at the experiences I was going through. I cannot say I was unhappy but restless, a sense of impatience.

*Well you knew you hadn't got the full picture, I presume?*

Yes. Looking back I realise this was what was wrong. At one point I thought they're hiding it from me, they don't think I'm ready to understand it. I quickly realised this was myself hiding it from me, not anyone else. I

151

found I only got the right answers when I asked the right questions.

*There's a lot hidden in that, isn't there?*

And at one time I got a little bit annoyed at this but was told until I knew the right question how could I understand the answer? It would seem that I had been through a very difficult period, it wasn't and yet it was, in the sense that I was playing tug-of-war with myself. For a period I remained still intensely interested in the things that I had left behind to be done in this world, also of course in those I loved. There was the urge to communicate with you and others but slowly this began to diminish as if I was distancing myself or being distanced by what I was learning and understanding.

*Out-growing it.*

Still the sense of *déjà vu* returned now and again and sometimes I think this was the most irritating of all, glimpses from a past longer than my life here in your world. The sense of elation, of ecstasy, started to be replaced by a sense of urgency, as if I needed to know more, almost a hunger for more.

There was then a period where I just went about absorbing all I could learn, trying to ask the right questions. I had a period where I watched the new arrivals coming, and understood more my own experiences. As you know, we had two friends who came over at that period. But slowly I found myself becoming more and more alone, by my own choice. It wasn't that I didn't spend time with others but there were periods where I had to withdraw to think things out, to lay out my treasures of knowledge, and try and fit the pieces together. During this period I was as active, if not more active, mentally than I have ever been in your world. There was no stress

152

to it, but this hunger and urgency. Someone over here suggested a new born child, a child coming into your world feels the same sense of urgency to arrive. Quite a good description of the feeling although the feeling of the child that is about to arrive is purely physical; it's the same feeling mentally. There are periods here which my friend and I, and others, have experienced in this world where for a moment we get a glimpse, and everything fits into place and we feel we know everything at that point and then it is gone. That is so much stronger over here and lasts, and it feels longer and so the urgency too. To have it there permanently is the hunger. I hope I have described this?

*Yes very well.*

Now, as you know, I have learned that my ties with your world are slowly being broken. Sometimes there is a feeling of guilt over this, a feeling of being selfish but not just with the ties that I am moving away from in the earth world, but also those I know where I am now. My surroundings, which seemed so clear cut and very much like your world at first, now are not so clearly defined but this I am told represents my state of mind.

*Do you feel that being a loner makes for guilt?*

No, but one has attached oneself to so many people with bonds of friendship and love, you feel you are turning your back on them. Does this answer your question?

*Yes. So it suggests it's a temporary sort of guilt only?*

Almost as if you are being a little ruthless in your pursuit.

*Yet you have no real choice I suppose? Except a very temporary one.*

153

Oh I have choices at this stage and they can last as long as I wish them to, but however long they last they are temporary.

*I want you to tell me before you finish this what are the real points of difference from your expectation when you were writing about the subject so much on earth, and what you really found. In a kind of way you've covered it and in another way not so much so from the Spiritualistic point of view.*

I expected to see those who had helped us on earth as guides, this I did see and so I was not disappointed in this. I did expect them to play a bigger part but they said, no, not now.

*In a way you weren't ready for them? To the level at which they wanted to speak now?*

Yes, that explains it precisely. I have now to reach up to them whereas in the past they reached down to me. That I did not expect.

*So they were being ruthless in their way too?*

They said it would encourage me to stay on the level I came over. Remember the ones who stay on that level are usually ones who have not been involved in the work that you and I have been involved in. Our relatives and friends mainly have lived their lives without this other contact. And so for them there is no feeling of let-down.

*Yes. So what you and I have studied over here has for you borne its fruit in that it made you ask questions earlier?*

Yes, and going by some of the people you and I both know who have also been involved in this work, they are almost equally divided between those who also ask questions earlier and those who still have not got round to asking.

*So we can make very different uses of this knowledge whilst we are on earth?*

Yes. There are some of our old colleagues, people we have known, who have gone further, much further than I myself and, I hate to say it, more quickly. There are however others who have come over here with the false impression of being guides and helpers, not realising that what they did in your world has not really prepared them for the world they are now in.

*In other words they wanted to sit a bit too high up the marriage table?*

Yes, very much so.

*Am I right that you've got quite a lot more of this to tell me next time?*

Yes. I have tried to think it through carefully for this session. I am also hoping that you, as you have done in the past, will point out where there are maybe gaps that I have missed and that need more explaining. So we will both work together on this.

## TWENTY-FIVE

## 11TH JUNE 1986

I have thought of what I spoke with you about and realise that there have been certain omissions, although to my mind some of them were obvious omissions, so obvious that they did not seem like omissions. The feeling of well-being that even though you expect it is much greater than one realises. This I think I omitted to speak of.

*You just touched briefly.*

The fact that your thoughts and feelings for people draw you to them without any conscious effort of going there. The difficulty which I still experience, which I am still experiencing, regarding time when I try to relate it to your world.

*A common problem.*

So our meeting now is in the future of the first one ahead of it. If I had not the knowledge that we had spoken on this subject previously, I would have had difficulty perceiving which was the past and which the future. I do not know if I am explaining this very well.

*Well, the very fact is hard for us to take up isn't it?*

Yes, because for me it does seem we are carrying on a conversation that has not had much of a break between. Yet the time sense I have learnt in this level has made me realise that time has passed. Whether this time sense will stay with me much longer I do not know, for I am beginning to realise that I can be in two times at once.

*Two times?*

Not just two places, and so you can see my difficulty.

*How much division of consciousness does this bring about?*

Not as much as I would have expected. The difficulties were at first, when I began to become aware of what I was doing. Then there was a confusing period.

*Is this what you meant by feeling not adjusted?*

Yes. As you know you and I both realised that there would be the ability to be in two places at once but we did not realise this could also tie in with time also. As I speak to you now, I have already done it.

*That's a puzzler to me obviously.*

But I am also doing it. Words are so clumsy. I have tried to think of ways to explain it to you. The nearest I can come to explaining it is by speaking of those people who can go to sleep at night and witness events happening on ahead, maybe months or weeks later. In the past I, and I suspect you, have always thought of the spirit travelling on in time.

*Yes, odd not to.*

Leaving the shell in the other time sense but not the spirit. (§ He says do you understand?]

*I'll have to think about that one.*

However, I now am beginning to understand that the spirit can inhabit both these time phases simultaneously and so the dreamer is not empty while the spirit travels on but merely inhabiting two time levels with more consciousness of the future time level. [§ It is the best way he can explain it.]

*So that's how precognition comes about is it?*

Yes.

*But you're obviously speaking of something much wider than just precognition?*

Yes. This is the only thing I could think of that would slightly explain what I have started becoming aware of. It appears to me now to be something I can accept, almost as if I knew it already. It would also take our friend Myers' theory a step further, as if he saw part of the picture but not the whole picture. How will you explain this to others? I do not know, I am having difficulty explaining it to you. Yet Peter says you should be able to grasp the essence because I discussed it with you.

*I see, yes.*

It would appear our spirit does not just inhabit different areas of space simultaneously but also time.

*Well we speak of the space–time continuum as if they were parts of the same thing.*

And from what I am experiencing now, they are. I have wondered if this could be why in the past on your level there has been difficulty understanding such words as fate or destiny. Is a thing pre-determined? Or do we have free will? As you know there have been many levels of thought on this.

*Yes indeed.*

I think it could go part of the way to explaining certain

things but I'm still working it out myself. I have given you a knotty problem to ponder.

This was a serious omission but I know I had doubts about my ability to explain it to you.

*And doubts about the reader's ability to understand it?*

Correct. However our friend said it could be left with you and you would resolve it.

*So these are also my preparatory lessons before going over?*

You could call them that. As you know I am still experiencing some difficulty in stepping back from my earthly ties. I feel I am partly able to do this. I know I need the detachment necessary, as if they are chains on my feet holding me down.

*I suppose the essence of it is that it should come about naturally, even though you have to give attention to it and effort and intention.*

Yes this is so.

*Like the apple falling from the tree at the right moment.*

But there is such an urge to go on. Yet one knows that while these attachments remain you are held by them.

*But if you shake the tree too soon the apple doesn't come down.*

When have I ever been a patient man?

*This is your theme song.*

It is something I am trying to learn. I still meet with those who would teach both you and me, though not on a regular basis. Almost it seems to me that when an interesting question occurs and it has to be the right one,

159

they, or one of them is there to give that little bit of help, not the complete answer but enough to spur me on towards it. My surroundings now seem to be more clear. There was a period when they were misty, confused impressions. I have learned to realise such periods are caused by myself as my perceptions change. I once described it to someone over here as needing new spectacles every so often. I know you will understand what I mean by this.

*Yes I do.*

I did not make the error of supposing anyone was doing this, but realised it was of my own doing. And so for the moment my surroundings seem clear and stable. Like you if I need trees I am where there are trees, if I need different terrain I am there. Sometimes it seems to me I sit within a beautiful golden glow; I say sit, rest might be a better word.

*And do you absorb more during that resting time?*

Yes.

How much time passes I'm never aware of. As I said earlier I am mixing still with others, not so much my relatives now, but others of like mind. One of my new-found travellers when in your world was from India and we have discussed the fact that slowly we seem to be spending periods of time alone, separately alone. I have noticed it and he had also noticed this. We have speculated on the reasons why we are doing this. He seems to feel that this is preparatory to that state of being when Holy Men in India went off by themselves, but they did it in your world. He feels he is heading in that direction, I don't know about me. I did not know him on earth but have found that we are fellow travellers at the moment. He seems to be going by certain teachings that

160

he followed when in your world. And of course I have listened – but will he be encountering things because he expects them to be that way?

*Same old problem.*

Yet he does admit to certain experiences similar to my own. Now we have to decide, my friend, whether these experiences were expected by us or whether they are genuine experiences that the spirit has to go through. There does seem a similarity in his experiences.

*So that points to their being objective?*

Yes. I knew you would grasp this point. Now however he expects to be what we would have called on earth a hermit, or to live for a period a hermit-like existence. I do not know if this will happen because he expects it, or because his teachers may be right, and this is the next step. I am leaving my options open and regret a little bit that he has said this to me, in case it has coloured now what I will feel and see. I do have the feeling that I am giving you some controversial stuff.

*Well all philosophic stuff is controversial in a way, isn't it?*

Not from your angle but from the angle that others will see it.

*You mean it'll go against their present comfortable view of things?*

Yes. They will not like to hear of my struggles.

*Then they're a bit wanting in spirit aren't they?*

No, they merely wish to have an end of struggling when they leave your level. Forgetting that the Ancient said 'As above, so below.' [§ I asked him what Ancient said

161

this and he said you would understand.] I have found some of my heroes. Sadly unheroic over here and you know I refer to those whose academic qualifications and intelligence I admired. It is surprising how many of them have this blind spot, as if their learning has left them moribund, stuck. It is a very disillusioning thing, for one would have expected them to have gone further than this.

*Hard for them to learn in a different field.*

Some of them seem like records playing the same tune again and again and so I would say to your readers: whatever you do, be flexible, be prepared to consider all possibilities, close your mind to nothing. To be an expert in one field is not enough. Someone told me recently, and I won't tell you who, that science fiction writers do very well over here. I think it's like a joke. The closed mind is your biggest stumbling block. I am relieved that mine was not so closed, nor yours, my friend, or we could not have this conversation. I do not think I have made many more omissions of the beginning stages of my sojourn here. You will notice that I am moving our medium more on to my speech level.

*Yes. She's got the essential qualities in good measure.*

This is why those who knew me did not understand my simplistic form of speaking in our beginning stages. Only with constant and deeper contact was there the opportunity to guide the medium more strongly.

I must confess in the early stages to a fear that reincarnation lay ahead of me. My feelings on this subject were very mixed, and as you know there was no way I could be assured. Whether this still lies ahead of me I do not know.

*The Old Gentleman doesn't tell you anything about this?*

162

He says I will understand later, it is too early to speak of this, but he did smile at my fear. I should so hate to lose this awareness and return again without the knowledge. At least this is how it appears to me.

*Yes. But once you were back here presumably you wouldn't miss it any more, because you wouldn't be aware of it?*

I agree but my awareness of what I know now is a precious thing, I would hug it to me.

*I don't think you'll be a hermit next time though.*

We shall see. However I leave my fears to one side now. I am pleased our meetings are going so well.

*Good. So am I.*

Although the medium was good, at one stage I despaired of explaining enough, that I would find the correct words and that she would receive them. However I feel we are both doing not too badly.

*Good. Next time are you going to continue the narrative, past your early days?*

I find these periods of being with you help me also to clarify my own thoughts.

*Well they're precious to me as I think you know.*

Who would have expected all those years ago, when we first met, that we would be doing this.

*Yes indeed.*

For we were not sure of each other then.

*No, not a bit.*

And although pursuing from different directions the

same cause, did not feel any great bond of affinity, far from it. At one point we had nothing to say to each other, beyond common politeness.

*I think it was the Survival Joint Research Trust days, curiously enough, which brought us together.*

Yes. Then we got each other's measure. Although at first neither of us expected the other to understand.

*Nothing like a common enemy is there?*

You are now one of the few, the very few, I can retain my contact with. My much loved Sylvia I cannot reach, only on a very basic level. My friends think it is not me.

*I think the kind of material you have been giving me will make many people feel it's not you because they are expecting more of the old Barbie.*

Did they really expect me to remain the same? I thought we knew better than this.

Earlier I spoke of my heroes. Unfortunately they have remained the same but it is not something they should have done. To have those who know me say this is not me, helps me understand that I am making progress for I would not be like those others I spoke of.

## TWENTY-SIX

## 14TH JULY 1986

Not much more progress to report, seem to be standing still. Find that this encourages in me a certain impatience. Find myself at times looking back to see how much progress has been made. Find it difficult to judge.

*I wouldn't think it possible for you to judge.*

You know I always try to do things other people wouldn't think of doing.

This medium is having difficulty with me today because I am projecting my thought.

*You mean it's a system that doesn't suit her quite so well?*

She likes to see me standing speaking to her. I'm not doing that today.

*I see. You're not giving her such a good anchor then?*

A different anchor. Also I wanted to use this means of communication to see how well it did. As you know experimentation is something I was always keen on. I still find my interest in the world I was involved in not very keen, flagging.

*Why is that?*

There is a dreamlike quality to it. Feel the mental and emotional links less strong. It is difficult to explain for

165

though I am interested in what you are doing and others, family and friends, there is this distance or distant quality.

*A detachment I suppose?*

Yes.

*Do you see it as a task or just as a fading interest?*

A fading interest and of course having agreed to work with you on this I see this as a task. Not an unpleasant one.

*When do you think you're going to be able to round it off?*

§ He's smiling.

When I myself am rounded off. There is still this tremendous urge for knowledge.

There seem to be no souls on this level that are reincarnating. I have checked back through my ancestors to see if any are missing. The line fades out. I can only presume, on the lower levels of awareness. As I suspected that the soul's return is almost a matter of form, I have looked among those who are more finely aware, and such is not the case.

*I wouldn't have thought there was much kinship between you and your ancestors.*

No but I am ever the reporter, the investigator. This was not for my own personal benefit.

*Are you saying really that none of our common friends in this Movement have, as far as you know, yet reincarnated?*

§ Correct but also that some of his ancestors seem to be missing. He's smiling at this, but says this is going back quite a few generations!

166

Which is why this medium never finds an uncle, a grandfather missing as a result of reincarnating. She would have to go further back to notice gaps in the families. With such people as I have discovered missing there seems to be part of them both here and in your world.

*In a dim kind of way I understand.*

But the spirit as an entirety is missing. I'm trying to keep this as simple as possible. As you know my family links are broken now or almost, although I would not be unkind to those of my family who still hold on to these links. Many of them do, but I was intrigued, and tried to find if there was a pattern, and a certain amount of earthly time before the return of a spirit. And it is easier to check along the links where there have been old earthly ties than to do it with those who do not know you.

*Would you say that all of our peers who are over on your side accept reincarnation as an obvious fact now, or is it not so?*

No. There are many who discuss it over here much as you do there. This is why I went on my exploration and of course what adds to the confusion is the residue that is left over here, for the whole spirit does not return. [§ He asks if he's becoming complicated again, Paul?]

*Well I've often been taught that only a small part of us is on the earth really so this is not so difficult for me.*

§ He says a small part of our awareness.

*Does he mean the nucleus remains in the other world?*

§ Yes.

*So it's like meeting the circumstances required to learn a missing chapter or isn't this what he's talking about?*

167

Yes. To complete the melody, to finish that which is unfinished, to refine that which is unrefined. Yes, this is what I mean.

*It's still a puzzle to me that reincarnation isn't more widely accepted. I can see that there would be obstinate people or people still carrying on with old earth ideas but I would have thought that to most it would have been an open and acceptable thing.*

Unpleasant truth.

*Unpleasant? That's a surprise. Is that why it's harder for many to accept the idea?*

Yes. Unpleasant to realise the soul goes through a series of lives. To accept they would have to give up the strong sense of their own identity.

*Yes I see.*

Unpleasant truth.

*So this growing lack of interest might be one of the steps necessary before you come back, or before you go on, whichever it is?*

Yes.

*A disentangling basically?*

Now you have it. [§ He seems pleased as if you've linked it.]

*Good.*

Putting my thoughts into words becomes more clumsy for me now. This is not just the medium's fault but my own. Thought is such an easier and clearer way of working.

168

*It's like thinking about a book which is very pleasurable before you actually have to get down to writing it?*

Yes. Sometimes I find the words so inadequate to explain. I did think you would find interest in my research into reincarnation. Certainly it is not easy to discover, almost as if there is a fading away and then rebirth. Not at all like queuing up in a doctor's surgery waiting to come down.

*What about the other aspect of it, getting to know more about your past lives. When does that come about?*

I'm waiting on this happening.

*You've had glimpses, or made guesses, no doubt?*

Some educated, some not, but I refuse to bore you with the details until I'm more sure of my ground.

*Right. And this could all be part of the detaching process I imagine? Detaching from the most recent one?*

I think this is possibly why I must do this. There is so much to learn. Sometimes I am appalled at how much.

*And you're no sluggard either are you?*

I feel a frenzy growing within me. Then I'm told to move more slowly by old teachers with whom you and I both have links. They say I will give myself indigestion and anyway it can only be learned gradually. I decided to do this exploration by myself. You would be surprised how few have thought of doing this over here, yet I would have thought it would be logical to do so, and I refer of course to some of our old friends and colleagues. Which makes me wonder if they deliberately do not wish to know.

*Not just yet perhaps.*

Certainly there are missing bits in the family tree, missing souls, or souls that are not quite as they should be, as if one is dealing with a shadow almost and not the substance and yet the substance is there. Very difficult to explain. I too am having my problems just as you are. The best way I can describe it is when I tried to link with such souls they seemed to be in a dreamer phase. The awareness was not total. There was a sharpness to certain of the ancestors.

*A sharpness to what?*

A sharpness, as if they were clearly defined. The personality was quite strong and clearly defined but in others there was a blurring and I realised this is what I was looking for.

*Which, the sharpness?*

No the spirits I contacted who seemed blurred round the edges of their personality.

*They were in a transitional state I presume?*

Yes. But they did not seem to be aware of this though I as an onlooker was aware of it. Therefore there is no conscious choice made although this may not be so in every case.

*Well there seem to be those who are really trying to speed up a bit and others who are content to accept whatever the normal pace is.*

Yes, two different types of reincarnation, not one. I called or have given one lot the name of the dreamers, the ones who seem to be returning unconsciously, and the others the ones who choose. There seem to be two distinct types.

*I'm certainly surprised that reincarnation is not so widely obvious as one would think.*

170

In the spirit world lack of investigation, lack of searching and I think at times a blinkered attitude. I too thought it would be more universally held.

*It seems that people are allowed to make their own pace, nobody seems to put a bomb under them.*

No, this is correct, no one interferes. You are allowed to be as lazy or as diligent as you wish. It can be irritating at times. One expects the teachers to pat one on the back and say well done.

*And they don't?*

No. You set your own lessons here.

*It's a more adult way of living after all.*

Can be frustrating, for one looks for approval from those you admire. This old habit dies hard. You are told that if this is of interest to you then you must deal with it, but the freedom of choice is there and no one says you should do this. The only advice I have had recently has been to avoid the danger of rushing things but that is all I have had.

*Yes. So quite a bit of what you might call the general man-made Spiritualistic picture, as distinct from what the teachers tell us, is really very premature and immature?*

Yes. But I can understand why this premise came about and so can you. We must have seemed really like children in the past. Carefully coaxed into making our own steps.

*Is the kind of distance that you feel towards the Old Fellow duplicated in how other mediums feel towards their teachers, Red Cloud and White Eagle and so on?*

I think the best description of it was given to me by one of our medium friends who described it as rather like a

171

mother with a child who coaxes the child to a certain stage of physical development, and then steps back and says now you must do the rest yourself. She understands it, says we would cling too closely to them. We would not do this in your world but over here it would be too easy. The way they have behaved with me is similar to others' experiences.

*So Peter's closeness when I pass over is likely to become more distant?*

Yes, because there will no longer be the need for such a strong contact between you. I admit I found it disappointing, but now realise the sense of it. It is like coming of age, although not quite.

*A Barmitzvah?*

Yes. I will come and speak with you again.

*It's been a difficult but salutary sitting. I think we must compliment the medium on being able to transfer it.*

It has been a little bit difficult but I felt she should get used to not having my visible presence which she has had at all of her other sittings.

*So this frees you to talk at a deeper level probably?*

Yes, but she did not expect it.

## TWENTY-SEVEN

# 18TH JULY 1986

§ Again he wants to work from a distance rather than to concern himself with showing himself to me.

As I look back at the conditions of my first period in spirit there was the relief and the elation of having successfully made the initial step over here. As you know one can know something in one's mind but the reality of the experience can sometimes be totally different.

*Indeed.*

And no matter how sure we think we are in our knowledge of what to expect there is always the small or large doubt in our mind that it will be completely different.

I know my description covered my initial passing.

*It reads extremely well.*

But there is difficulty in conveying the timelessness of the whole thing for when I speak to you I feel I have to speak in terms of time. The period that followed I have explained. I will not try to carry on from where I left off. If I overlap forgive me. How long one spends with relatives, or how long I spent with my relatives, I cannot judge but then came the pulling away. I can best describe it as meeting an old friend on your level with whom suddenly you find you have not very much in common,

173

even though you are pleased to see them. This was my experience with my relatives and with some of my friends, a feeling of pleasure that they looked well and seemed content, but a distance as if I was only passing through their level. Looking back I think this is what I was doing, the way you would pass down a street and chat before you carried on with your journey. Then it seemed I had passed beyond them, again the definition of a street would best be the way to describe this. During this period I felt keen excitement, I've always been one who liked looking round the next corner or over the next hill and was for a little while disappointed because there was no change that I could discover taking place.

*Taking place in you?*

Yes. I find you can only judge progress in retrospect, but not when it's happening, for the change is so insidious you are not aware of it, it does not rush over you, it creeps over you. I found myself speaking with people, some of whom I knew, some who were new to me and yet not new, as if I recognised them, although I did not know them here in your world. This at first seemed to me merely a change of people. I myself did not feel any different from the period where I had walked down the street. I'm using this to try and explain, speaking of it as travelling, rather than as layers of consciousness or awareness or levels which is more complicated.

*Here's the journalist in you.*

It's easier to visualise. And so I was in my new district. I lingered I think for a little while. I noticed I could now perceive a glow around people and yet this does not describe it. I seemed to be looking at people whom I was with in a totally different fashion. There was still the form of a physical body, but this seemed faded somehow,

174

whilst the glow or radiance around them became brighter and I seemed to be paying more attention to that than to the other. I found myself stopping sometimes by myself, evaluating and judging what was taking place and what was the reality of what I was seeing. Much the type of thing you do when in a foreign country and you are adapting. Some of these people seemed to me very good and sincere people, yet some seemed not to be questioning or looking further, as if they felt they had arrived.

*But they still had the glow?*

Yes. These people had a stronger awareness than the people I had left. With the ones I had left, I had found difficulty in communicating unless on a general level. These people I was now with had a more refined consciousness, more awareness. Some did not wish to mix but seemed to be lost in their own world of thought. Others as I say seemed to have no curiosity but were content to be just there. There seemed to be a contentment, almost in some cases a lethargy. I seemed to stay longer at that level or district. There was a feeling of being extremely comfortable with oneself yet I knew that I had to be on my guard against becoming too comfortable. It was difficult, for the feeling of resting from labours, of a job well done, this type of feeling, was there. One could almost feel the will to go on becoming weakened. How long I remained in this state I still am not sure of, but it was a long period I think, for I seemed to 'blink' in and out of it. There were periods when I was aware that I must move on and other periods where I did not feel this urge. It is amazing how fascinating the pattern of your life is when looking back at it.

*You mean your life in particular?*

175

All of us. One could always lose oneself in it, watching how this pulled you this way, that influenced you that way, also there was beginning the urge to look beyond that life to the one that was previous. It was as if you did not have enough time to think. Does this sound strange?

*It sounds strange.*

There seemed so much to think about.

*In other words life was going at a quicker pace really than on earth?*

In a sense yes. I cannot say I was day-dreaming at this point but it was similar to it. I felt my awareness of the urge to go on to learn more was fading. I realise looking back that there was no temptation in remaining on the first stage. Temptation started to come at the second stage. Temptation to linger and to say: it's enough that I am here.

*Your spiritual deck chair?*

Yes. Strangely, once I pulled myself away from this district, my dreaminess, my lolling in the spiritual deck-chair, I sharpened mentally immediately. It was like coming awake again. It was like getting cold water thrown in your face, then and then only could you judge what had happened previously, but not while you were experiencing it. Almost I felt myself dragging myself away from that stage or district but once I had made the effort then I was alert, I became aware and very much sharper. Now I took more notice of my surroundings; whereas things had been hazy, now they were more defined. The shape of those I met seemed to consist of more light than anything else, or else I was seeing the light clearer. I tried to rid myself of this notion, to say to myself there should be no shape. I find this bit difficult to explain to you, for I was still

176

perceiving others as having similar shapes to the physical envelopes they had left behind.

*So you could know it was Percy or Henry or whoever it was.*

Some I could not have defined as man or woman but a combination of both.

*That's interesting.*

So I did not know if they were Henry or Henrietta or a combination of both. This I had not been aware of in the other stages, but I told you I was seeing clearer now. I tried to look beyond the physical shape they seemed to show me, reminding myself that I could be seeing this because I was giving them this shape. [§ And he asks if you understand?]

*Yes. Your problem you've named so often.*

But it still persisted. And so I think it was a combination of my inability to rid myself of the idea that they should have shape and form, but possibly also their idea that they should have shape and form. So a combination. We all seemed very busy, talking, sharing, and helping each other with experiences we had been through, almost it seemed to me as a reaction to the other level we had just left. [§ He asks again if you understand?]

*Putting on a spurt because of lost time as it were.*

Yes. Stop me if you do not understand. I find these words so inadequate to explain. But yes, as if we were trying to make up for a slothful period or a period of spiritual laziness. I found most of these people, some of whom I recognised – one who was a medium friend of ours – could not remember or could not judge how long it

177

had taken to pass through that period. Some speculated that we needed the rest, that maybe it was a delayed action. Some speculated that this betrayed a weakness in ourselves to pat ourselves on the back. This is what I mean when I say we talked and tried to help each other. All may have been the reasons or none but I feel that some were the reasons. For looking back it seemed to me a period of complacency, almost of spiritual superiority.

*You're talking now of the beginning of this new stage, or are you back in the stage before?*

The state before. For this stage or district that I was now in seemed more hurtful with its sharpness and its demand for examination of self.

*This sounds like the mental world.*

We seemed, all of us, to be again examining ourselves, which we had not done at that previous level, our senses seemed heightened and sharpened and more critical. There was no complacency now, rather a period of re-evaluating, trying to understand. It was at this period we got some help from the teachers. I think they thought we would chase ourselves into a corner. And so there was a stepping in. They spoke of remembering we were ridding ourselves of certain aspects carried deep within our natures, our spirits, almost like remnants we had carried over from earth. This gave us some help. They spoke of many people being fooled by this level, but that they fooled themselves, that instead of tearing ourselves to bits in our evaluation we should feel pleased we had started to move again and turn our thoughts outward instead of inward. This was not easy to do, we seemed to be in an orgy of self criticism. I realise this is why they felt they had to step forward. It was such a sharp change from the other, as if we had swung to the other extreme. We felt

178

such fools that we had fooled ourselves. Slowly some of us were able to continue our journey but much chastened, not so confident, others still continued in the circle of introspective criticism. The best example I can think of is going back into history where certain people indulged themselves in flagellation, but this was the mental kind. But, our teachers told us, just as dangerous to our progress as the other level we had left. I think looking back we took almost as long on this level as we did on the other. Certainly it would seem that this was so. I could not have believed I would have wallowed, and I use this word deliberately, in such self-criticism, almost taking pleasure in it.

Now you know why I used to come and speak of difficulties, but at the time could not speak of what was happening to me for I had not the perspective to see it and speak of it properly.

Now there seemed to be a quieter period, a resting period, the way one would rest after a battle. I look back at that period and see myself exhausted, almost drained. Of course the teachers were no longer there now. They may have been there for those who still remained caught in this trap of their own criticism, but we were no longer aware of them. Now seemed to come a period of resting, of summing up what we had been through, a period of realising again we had escaped from another self-inflicted trap. You can understand why we felt this tiredness. We seem to withdraw from each other now more by mutual consent. There was not the mixing that there had been on the other levels or districts. I do not like the word level, it implies going up or down. This is why I try to call it districts which means you are going across rather than up or down.

*Districts on the same level?*

179

Yes. I do not mean we were unfriendly to each other but we seemed to need more space from each other, yet we were not solitary. While I could look back at the other two periods or districts and be a little bit ashamed and annoyed with myself, this level evokes only pleasant memories, as if I was pulling myself together. I did not notice change in the people around me, only in the fact that we became more apart, with more space between us. And so I cannot say my awareness showed me great changes, the changes seemed to be in our distance rather than in the people or the way we were viewing things. I think we were consolidating what we had learned so far. I started to become impatient; what was I doing, where was I going? Doubts crept into my mind, was this also in its own way a trap I was inflicting upon myself? But there was within me the urge to continue and so I reasoned that this could not be a trap I was inflicting upon myself or there would not be the urge to continue.

*Presumably these people you were with now, from whom you were gradually becoming a little bit more distant, these would be people at the same spiritual level, broadly speaking?*

Yes, in fact we seemed more in tune than in the other districts I had been in, yet this district seemed to be the period where we pulled away.

*But essentially you were closer to these people than any you may have met before?*

One felt one did not need to be with the other person to be with them. When I say solitary I do not mean alone, there was great harmony between us, much stronger than at any other period with others I had been with, almost as if we did not need to share thoughts with each other, for it would have been like sharing thoughts with yourself.

*About how many would there be in this group, if you can call it such?*

There seemed to me not many, maybe thirty, maybe more, but not that many.

*So it's like a team in a way?*

Possibly.

## TWENTY-EIGHT

## 3RD SEPTEMBER 1986

I spoke to you last time of districts. The *appearance* of districts was how I felt of them at that period. Looking back now, of course I realise they were stages in the soul's progress; that actually I never moved anywhere but at the time there seemed to be the appearance of moving from one area to another. I cannot name the exact period when I came to understand that they were stages of awareness, layers of myself that I was peeling away. Let us say it seemed to me the awareness slowly crept over me.

*Good way of putting it.*

And as it did so [§ he keeps saying words are so difficult and that he has to get his context right] – this awareness, that crept over me, gave me new understanding of what I had been through. I realised that this also was a new phase of understanding, that I was already moving back from the experience and evaluating it. And so during what I had called the passive district, the passive level, when I look back at the critical period, and, as you put it, the spiritual deck-chair period, although it seemed I was passive I was still learning and going onwards. For the evaluation was also a period where I took the experiences, as you take a jigsaw puzzle and put it together. Some pieces were still missing but the picture was beginning to emerge. As I said earlier, during this

182

period my awareness of others around me was that there did not seem to be so many on my level that I was aware of, nor did we mingle but seemed to withdraw in perfect understanding.

*Like the Indian you told me about?*

Yes. It was rather like being in the company of someone you have known for a long time and there is no need to talk, silence is also companionable. This is the best way I can describe it, where there was complete understanding and no need to communicate. I felt if I had communicated during this level, during this period, there would have been nothing we could have helped each other with, as our experiences were basically similar. And so we were at a period of judging and examining our experiences. The Indian I spoke of earlier, or the soul that had been Indian – I use this word only for identification purposes – fascinated me because this soul seemed to be ready to move on and as I too was looking for my directions, I watched with great interest his next mental leap. He seemed to be going through a period of great mental struggle which he could not seem to communicate to the rest of us. This also seemed rather ominous to the rest of us as obviously representing the next stage; that his anguish was real, yes, that his soul was great, yes, but we found it difficult to comprehend how this was coming about. There seemed to be both an agony and an ecstasy to it. He referred to it as a purging process and I wondered if this had links back in his previous life with certain religious principles he had been taught, or whether it would apply to all of us.

Whatever happened I cannot say for sure because suddenly the communication and rapport we had was gone. I cannot say if he went anywhere, only that we were no longer aware of him. I have to be so careful about my

183

words, going away, levels, time. The concepts are difficult. I do know that there seemed no longer to be a way of communicating with him and can only presume that he had reached the next stage.

I did notice, however, before this stage he had – words again – turned totally inward and seemed to be unaware, during the latter period, of our presence. He reminded me, during this period, of the classic example of a mystic, a fervour and intensity was unmistakable, also a sort of exultation. I could not see myself going through such a phase.

*Maybe you will in terms of your different temperament.*

And I wondered how it would affect me. During this period the curse of time was upon me, I kept trying to work out how long things had lasted, which I discovered later can only confuse and muddle the soul who is doing so. But you'd be surprised how such a silly habit as this can persist, knowing I was in timelessness, yet trying to work out the periods I had spent so far.

*Very human isn't it?*

Yes but I expected to get rid of such habits more easily when the body was no longer there. How much this delayed me I am not sure.

*Well, delay's only a question of time again.*

I will use the word blocked. This is a better word. But in your terms it was a form of delay. Then I too gave up this fruitless task, and again spent my energies on evaluating and judging my experiences so far. At this period I was aware that we would be doing this, that which we are doing today, and because I realised this, spent more energy compiling my report. I must admit at this period to a feeling of impatience and some resentment.

184

*At having to do it you mean?*

Yes. But then resolved it by accepting the fact that as we were going to do it, I had already compiled this report. On your level it is not as complicated as that. Destiny to most of your level is something that is not seen but that you walk blindly towards. On this level it is more difficult because you are inhabiting two periods, two spaces. And so I paid attention and revised what I had experienced. Then I seemed to feel, and I can only describe it in physical terms, a quickening, almost as if my mental processes were speeding up. [§ He asks if you understand this, Paul?]

*Yes. Rather like the physical exhilaration on a mountain top?*

Yes. This is why I have to explain it in physical terms. There was a sense of urgency. I can best describe it as an iron filing being drawn towards a magnet. This is the best physical description I can give, the pull, the urging. I do not know if I looked exulted or mystical during this period. I would rather say I got excited. I realise now why that other soul turned inward and became unaware of the rest of us, for I too felt fascinated by what was taking place. If I could liken it to anything other than the magnet and the iron filing, I would liken it to being born. It is how I imagine the spirit would feel as it rushes into the world. I can only say this is how it felt, almost as if conditions, events were taking over and drawing you along with them. And so there was no time to pay attention to others, only to look inwardly and be fascinated by what was taking place. [§ He seems to be doubting that he is explaining this.]

*Yes, I think I'm with him.*

At one point there was the feeling that I could have

185

been split asunder, again the likening to birth. When I was next able to pay attention to my surroundings, I looked for differences in myself and at first was most disappointed because there seemed to be no difference, yet what I had gone through surely I felt should have made some dramatic difference.

*Were you still surrounded by your peers?*

No, they seemed more distant.

*So that was parallel to the experience of the Indian as far as you could tell?*

It seemed so. And there was a feeling of being alone, not lonely but alone. I felt a little bit at a loss, yet I did not feel uncomfortable. Later I was told by those you and I know who have spoken to us in the past, that not everyone experiences this and feels comfortable. There seemed no one that I could use as a reference point to myself. You understand? Rather like being adrift in space. I was alone with only myself as company. I must admit, at this period, to a stage of patting myself on the back for being so comfortable with myself, then of course I worried about it! I realised after a while this was the natural next stage, total individuality, with no links to hold you solid, only yourself. I also realised during this period how not only on this level but on my passing to spirit, I had used people's views and knowledge of me to reinforce me. Now if you will forgive the physical expression, I stood alone.

Although the experience was exhilarating I felt uneasy with it, not uncomfortable, uneasy, like being in solitary confinement.

*Yes. Sounds to me as if there's more of it to come. I don't mean the solitary confinement, I mean the total experience you are describing.*

186

I cannot describe it as a limbo period because it is not. This is the period I am now at. And so my story so far has ended. Even as I am speaking with you, you seem a long way away, while at the same time I am conscious of you and the medium. And so my aloneness is still around me although I speak to you.

*Are you going to add to the story from a journalistic point of view or do you want it to end here?*

I do not know how long we can keep this link going. From my old thinking I never liked leaving stories without endings. However I am treading on unknown ground. Let us say I will keep the link going as long as I can.

Of course I need not tell you that it is a projection of myself that the medium has been seeing. I am no longer capable of doing this although I know there have been reports of my presence with others over the last period.

Also I am finding it difficult, extremely difficult, to remain interested now in the things and people that would normally have concerned me. I can see by your thoughts that in physical time I have not been long over here.

*No that's right.*

Yet it seems aeons.

*Really?*

Aeons.

*Yes. Because you measure it in richness of experience?*

I was most surprised to learn the shortness of the period. I merely thought you were ageing well, but realise now very little time has passed. I have spoken with those you and I both know, Peter and the Old Man. They still do not give much away. Their reason for speaking with me was because I had sent out a plea for just a little bit of

187

help. There was even a period of panic where I wondered if I was going in the right direction. It was during such a short, brief period of contact that they spoke of some souls' inability to accept this aloneness. Their words of comfort were that one must achieve identity, before it is lost. And then they reminded me of the others we have known in the past who had to separate themselves from people.

*In past lives you mean?*

No. Others, other highly evolved souls that have walked the physical level who withdrew from those around them to attain greater awareness, that this was a necessary process.

*I take it you are not much interested in what effect this book will make on people in the Spiritualistic world?*

I am trying to be interested. No, I am not very interested. Yet I saw myself as doing this and so it must have its place in the scheme of things.

*It's a necessary postlude isn't it? And a corrective.*

If it is not rejected.

*Will be by many, I don't doubt!*

I can see changes in my personality, character, essence. I do hope I never become bland.

*Not much chance of that I think.*

For it is someting I would abhor.

*Do you suppose that when this particular phase has completed itself you'll begin to join up with knowledge of your former lives more fully?*

I hope so.

188

*And what about the spiritual group to which essentially you belong?*

We have spoken of this here. When that stage is reached I do not know.

*But you certainly won't be communicating then I imagine?*

If it is possible I would.

*Yes. It's surprising to me that Myers, Gurney, Doyle, Lodge and so on don't seem to have changed all that much.*

I can only presume they have wished to retain that contact.

*As of a work undone perhaps, or not completed.*

Not completed. Trying to use others to finish it off.

*So for them too a postlude in a way?*

Yes. You have no questions for me, my friend?

*I don't want to go on to questions that are irrelevant or foolish.*

I understand. Be assured that this state is not uncomfortable; that it bears a resemblance to the hermit within his cell, who denies himself contact for better understanding. Just as he is not uncomfortable, neither am I. I am not sure if this truly represents a stage or level unlike the others which now look to me like the layers one would pull off an onion. It seems to me quite a distance apart from those other experiences and I can only measure it by the distance I feel between myself and others now, which was not there before. I have also wondered if in the future it will be more difficult to communicate to you what I am experiencing.

*I've taken it as inevitable that such a situation will arise.*

Be assured if there is a way to speak of it I will try.

*That'll be fine.*

Again I do this, because I am already doing it, and I am beginning to wonder if we set this up at another time, another place, but were not aware of it, for it seems inevitable that we continue this as far as it can go.

*Yes. So we have a paradox that what happens to you out of time will need time down here?*

Yes. I have thought of what has been said in the past. The expression 'as above, so below' then makes sense, taken in that context. And so it would seem we live our lives in reverse.

*I don't quite follow what you mean here.*

I will try to explain. It is because of our paths joining as they have joined during these and future communications that they first joined in the past. [§ And he asks if you understand?]

*No I'll have to think about it.*

§ He says he will make one more attempt. Because of what has happened above, it led to what happened below.

*Yes, yes, I follow that of course.*

And so in reverse. I will leave now.

*Yes. God bless you and many thank yous to you.*

Give me time; when I am ready to communicate I will. [§ And he's gone.]

_____

*You had a very good contact, Marie, didn't you?*

§ It was like someone using full strength on you when they hadn't used it before, do you know what I mean? It was as if today he was using his spiritual muscle and for some reason he hadn't been using it before. It was quite overpowering, I think that is the word I want.

*But you didn't seem to find it hard to reproduce it.*

§ No but I felt as if somebody had my head in a vice. Do you know what I mean? It was like being in a vice mentally. I could almost feel myself thinking, 'Oh this is too strong', as if you've had these muscles all along but I didn't know you had. It was that kind of feeling. As if suddenly he was using those muscles.

*Very good indeed. And now I'll be able to complete the book, it's all ready, except for this finish.*

§ Barbanell didn't seem interested, Paul. He seemed almost to give a sort of mental shrug . . .

*Yes that's right. I didn't think he'd be interested in that part of it because his task was to produce the message; what happens to it is my problem.*

§ It's not something that really interests him.
That vice wasn't uncomfortable, it was just far more restrictive than he's been, you know?

*Well he didn't give you much latitude did he?*

§ No, no. He usually plays me lightly but today he was holding tight. That is the best way I could describe it.

191

# APPENDIX

APPENDIX

# 12TH SEPTEMBER 1986

*Note:* It will be seen that the main speaker acknowledged himself to be Cosmo Lang who, when Archbishop of Canterbury, suppressed the 'Churches' Report on Spiritualism and Communication'. The lady who is with him, yet stands apart from him, is shown to be Estelle Roberts. She explains why she has brought him.

§ I'm aware of a gentleman and lady now standing beside you. They're not standing together so I take it that it is important to say that they're not really together. The lady is a tall thin elegant lady. I've seen her before. She says she used to do what I did – what I do.

*Yes. I know who it is.*

§ And she's smiling at you and she's saying you did leave the door open.

*Yes I did indeed.*

§ She's wanting me to speak to the man. Very serious looking man. I don't feel . . . possibly he has got a sense of humour but he doesn't look as if he has. Rather distinguished looking. He's so formal with me, this man, very correct, very disciplined.

*I think he'd better unbend a little.*

195

§ Tells me his links were with the orthodox Church, and tells me he had a high position there.

*No wonder he's correct then.*

§ I don't know if he said Bishop or Archbishop, I only caught the 'Bishop' part so I'm not sure. Seems to be taking me to Yorkshire, so I don't know if he was born there or if this was something to do with his work.

*I don't feel as if I've known him personally.*

§ The lady brought him along. She says you would know *of* him. Would you understand this?

*Oh yes, much better.*

§ The lady is speaking. 'We are, all of us, interested in what you and Barbanell have been trying to do. It has helped not only your level of understanding but ours because we cannot really reach him. He always was a path maker and it is interesting to note that he hasn't changed. We missed his presence with us and realised something had taken place. Our friend here feels that the two of you have been going too deeply into this, that there are some things best unkown, which the human spirit must discover for itself. I thought you would be interested in his theory.'

*I'm all for making things known where I can.*

§ 'That is why I encouraged him to come and express these views to you. I thought you might like to know we have some dissenters among us. So I have brought our friend along, although we both only knew *of* him, to put his viewpoint but he seems strangely reluctant now that he has made the contact.'

*I suppose this is repeating old restraints?*

196

§ The gentleman's shaking his head. The lady says, 'I'm afraid our friend still thinks it is not right to penetrate the veil too far.'

He's speaking now: 'I think the soul's progress should be an individual one. And that it should be taken with trust, not attempting to see too far ahead but allowing what will happen to happen. Surely you will alter the progress of such souls who will read your book?'

*Only if they so desire, I'm helpless otherwise.*

§ 'And the experiences they will encounter over here then will be known to them.'

*It may prepare them a bit for it.*

§ 'But surely this is to make the path too easy?'

*It doesn't sound so, from their descriptions of it.*

§ 'I feel it is wrong for a blueprint to be given.'

*What is the Gospel but a blueprint?*

§ 'That can be interpreted in many ways. Yours would not be so. Surely the soul's progress blindly through those hazards forms the experience needed for refinement?'

*I don't think I'd quarrel with that.*

§ 'Yet your book will attempt to chart that which should remain uncharted until it is reached.'

*Well I would say it's not my chart, although I've attempted to reproduce it, but I can see no reason why it should be wrong to do so, nor have you given me one.*

§ 'I agree that when I was on your level, in certain spiritual matters I wore blinkers. I do not feel I do this now. Of course I may be in error.'

197

*I'm very glad you come to talk. I welcome you.*

§ 'But I feel, and one or two of my colleagues feel the same, that this is a dangerous road you walk with the one who gives you this information.'

*Wherein lies the danger?*

§ 'You may rob the soul of its initiative, of its opportunity to trust and walk only with that.'

*You trust in another way. He could not have undergone those experiences he tells of without a very real trust.*

§ 'But by explaining them to the souls who follow there will not be the need for trust.'

*There'll still be the need for trust, it may be at a better level, at a deeper level, than I can provide.*

§ 'I have not come thinking I could dissuade you. I have come merely to put another viewpoint. I do not think I could dissuade you but maybe I can give you pause, maybe I can make you hesitate just a little and think again.'

*It's very unlikely.*

§ 'I accepted this but felt I must still do it. Maybe you are right and I am wrong, maybe the blinkers I thought I had removed still remain.'

*Whichever of us is right or wrong I don't think it'll make too much difference. It's still very much for each soul to work out his own destiny is it not?*

§ 'But think of it, if each level is known for the difficulties it will give the soul, will not the soul say, "Aha, I know this, I know how to move on from this"?'

*No I think the soul will say I must work harder because*

*these are going to be very difficult experiences which will search me out.*

§ 'Therefore you would not feel it better for the soul to experience these things as unknown factors?'

*No because I think there are so many other unknown factors and anything that can strengthen the soul is worth while. And many say better to strengthen it here than have to do it there.*

§ 'I feel the strength of the soul comes from facing the unknown, you would make it known.'

*You never really make it known do you? You only make a tiny fragment of it known.*

§ 'It is something that disturbs me greatly.'

*You wouldn't go on an Arctic exploration without knowing what you could about it, though you certainly wouldn't know everything.*

§ 'But to know is to be prepared.'

*Why should we not be prepared if we can?*

§ 'The preparation of the soul for the passing to this world, this I can understand and accept, but then the way should be uncharted, just as the soul's life on your level was a blank page, no one presented the soul with a book mapping out the dangers and the difficulties. Didn't the soul achieve more?'

*It's a doubtful proposition with so much to achieve anyway.*

§ 'Let us take two souls born into your level, one knows the pitfalls, one must work blindly. To which is the greater achievement? Surely to the one who works

199

blindly for they have had to learn and experience and judge those experiences.'

*Well so has the other but at a rather different level perhaps. Surely it's the individual effort upon himself that counts at whatever level?*

§ 'Yes if both achieve the same.'

*Well they will eventually, will they not?*

§ 'Surely the greater glory, the greater understanding goes to the one who knew nothing?'

*It's only a question of a degree of a few years as to when he begins to know is it not? Perhaps it's his fault if he knows nothing, or partly so.*

§ 'I do not feel so. I feel that the soul is strengthened by facing the unknown, by walking blindly, by trusting, or an act of faith.'

*No! To me you are denying valuable experience to certain souls when you say 'Thou shalt not'. There are many ways to the Kingdom surely?*

§ 'Yes but most have to be sought by the soul itself moving in unknown territory.'

*Now there I think is the limitation that you are making. Whether it's known or unknown it's still the effort that's the point.*

§ 'You would see no added strength to a soul that pursued such a path?'

*This I wouldn't agree with. Help is given in all forms of life. It's a form of service which I'm sure you would not wish to deny.*

§ 'I do respect your motives for what you do. I know

the meaning, the intent is good. I do not come to rebuke you but to ask you, "Have you considered this other side that I present?" '

*It seems to belong so much to my past when as a Catholic I might have been more inclined to agree with you but not so now.*

§ 'So you would have no mysteries, nothing that the soul . . .'

*The mystery grows, it doesn't diminish with the extra knowledge, it grows, if knowledge it be.*

§ 'So you are saying the soul cannot be harmed by knowing too much before it is ready?'

*I don't think it can know it before it's ready. It will fail to perceive it. It can only receive according to the size of its own vessel.*

§ 'We, my colleagues and I, do not feel so. We feel the harm to the soul could be great because it is being given knowledge of its future experiences and the trap therein.'

*What harm can result?*

§ 'A trap is not a trap when it is known. Your colleague had difficulty with these levels because they were not known and so he met each experience as a new one.'

*May I ask if you accept reincarnation?*

§ 'I am unsure on this point.'

*Unsure, yes.*

§ 'I certainly have had no experience of it myself although I am trying to extend the boundaries of my

201

knowledge. I cannot give you a yes or no answer on this.'

*No. Very well then. I won't pursue my argument along that line.*

§ 'We do not fault you for your endeavours.'

*No, no I appreciate your being ready to say so, I do indeed.*

§ 'But we feel in your urge to help, to teach, that some things must be left unsaid.'

*Are you saying then that those who imparted this knowledge to me were at sin in doing so? It didn't come from myself.*

§ 'We think they have been mistaken, that their level, their knowledge of the level they are on is profound but that the level they would have you teach would misuse this knowledge and thereby the soul would not achieve its potential.'

*In any school, whether it's a kindergarten class or the sixth form, you are free to teach as much as you feel it's possible for the pupil to understand.*

§ 'Until now such knowledge has not been given. We are speaking of a different type of knowledge. There has been in the past, this we now acknowledge, the link up between the two worlds, but to follow that progress further to the point that has recently been reached by one of your colleagues, this has not been done before.'

*He, as I understand it, is subject to the law and we frequently find communicators say, 'This I'm allowed to tell you, that I'm not allowed to tell you.' So those who speak in this way admit and subject themselves to the law, the spiritual law as they so far understand it.*

202

§ 'We feel there has been a mistaken belief that more knowledge of the soul's progress is needed.'

*Would not the missionary who first approached a savage race say that the souls there needed more knowledge?*

§ 'Of a basic kind, yes.'

*Then who am I to limit the knowledge?*

§ 'There have been others who have known while living in your world, about these other experiences that the soul goes through. Why did they not speak of them?'

*Why indeed. Your implication is that they would say it was not lawful to do so, or if not lawful at least unwise.*

§ 'Unwise.'

*I must say that I prefer the wisdom of those who have already undergone or are undergoing some of these experiences to decide what the law allows them to tell us and for a good motive.*

§ 'Then we will agree to differ.'

*Yes. I fear it must be so. I'm very glad that you came and spoke so honestly to me.*

§ 'We felt we must. Your woman colleague offered to bring us so that we could express our views. For we felt that you had only heard one side, not the other and that we should serve as a note of caution, possibly not to stop you but to make you pause.'

*Maybe it would be good to convey what you have said in one of the Christian magazines to those who are interested in this subject as orthodox Christians?*

§ 'If you wish to use my words you are welcome.'

203

*Thank you. Is it permitted to ask your name or do you prefer not to give it?*

§ 'You know who I am.'

*I know your probable rank but no more than that.*

§ 'There was a period when you could have said I was your enemy. Does this help?'

*Yes it does. If I said Cosmo would I be right?*

§ 'Yes. I will leave you to your friend.'

*Yes, thank you very much.*

§ The lady now says, 'I knew you would be interested to hear from him.'

*Very much so, yes.*

§ 'I knew it would give you pleasure to discuss this attitude and I decided to make the sitting interesting.'

*Well you certainly did. It was a job to get his name out from him wasn't it?*

§ 'He wanted to be judged by his words rather than to pull rank as he called it.'

*Yes, well that was fair.*